BY
LOVING
OUR OWN

17.95

George Grant
(Used with the kind permission of William Christian.)

BY LOVING OUR OWN

George Grant and the Legacy of Lament for a Nation

Carleton University Press
Ottawa, Canada
1990

edited by **Peter C. Emberley**

ISBN 0-88629-133-X (paperback)
ISBN 0-88629-132-1 (casebound)

Printed and bound in Canada

Carleton Library Series 161

Canadian Cataloguing in Publication Data
Main entry under title:
By loving our own

(The Carleton Library ; CLS 161)
ISBN 0-88629-132-1 (bound)
ISBN 0-88629-133-X (pbk.)

1. Grant, George, 1918- . 2. Nationalism--
Canada. 3. Canada--History--1963- .
4. Technology--Social aspects--Canada. 5. Political
science-- Philosophy. I. Emberley, Peter C. (Peter
Christopher), 1956- . II. Series.

FC97.B9 1990   971   C90-090263-9
F1034.2.B9 1990

Distributed by Oxford University Press Canada,
                70 Wynford Drive,
                Don Mills, Ontario,
                Canada. M3C 1J9
                (416) 441-2941

Cover design: Aerographics Ottawa

Acknowledgement

Carleton University Press gratefully acknowledges the support ex-
tended to its publishing programme by the Canada Council and the
Ontario Arts Council.

This book has been published with the help of a grant from the Social
Science Federation of Canada using funds provided by the Social
Science and Humanities Research Council of Canada.

Cover photograph used with the kind permission of William Christian

TABLE OF CONTENTS

ACKNOWLEDGEMENTS

Grateful acknowledgement is here expressed to Mrs. Ruth Bell who under the auspices of the Dick and Ruth Bell Lecture Series and to inaugurate the first of the series, provided funds which enabled participants to come to the conference at which these papers were delivered. I also thank the Social Sciences and Humanities Research Council, the British Council, the President, Vice-President (Academic), and Deans of Arts, Social Sciences, and Graduate Studies of Carleton University for their contributions. The Samuel and Saidye Bronfman Family Foundation and the Canadian Studies Directorate, Secretary of State generously funded the publication of this collection. The pictures of George Grant and that with Sheila Grant were taken by William Christian, who generously permitted their reproduction in this book. Alex Colville kindly offered to have "Truck Stop" and "Canadian 50-cent piece" appear in this collection.

It is not possible to thank everyone who helped with this manuscript. I would like, though, to single out my conference assistants Yasmeen Abu-Laban and Phil Azzie, who were tireless in their support and who made many perceptive suggestions; Tom Darby and Randy Newell for their helpful thoughts about the conference and the publication; Valerie Pereboom for her continuous administrative assistance; Jon Alexander for his technological expertise; and Claire Gigantes for her very fine editing. Finally, but especially, I am grateful to Mrs. Sheila Grant whose encouragement and enthusiasm were unflagging throughout.

PREFACE

They constantly try to escape
From the darkness outside and within
By dreaming of systems so perfect that no one
will need to be good.

T.S. Eliot

By loving our own. What a complex train of thought is conveyed by this seemingly elementary phrase! As a condensed proposition, Professor George Grant's words are startling in their simplicity. They seem to be, and have been taken to be, a formula for our complex destiny as a small and young nation, a nation buttressed by powerful ideological and technological forces whose transformative power denies the relevance of our nationhood. Yet, these words are more. They are as much a riddle, or a paradox, even a contradiction, as they are a nourishing prescription. For, by inviting us to love our own, Grant at the same time was indicating to us what made that love difficult, if not impossible.

Love, Plato taught us, is a complex passion. It can make us strong but it can also be a master and enslave us; it can elevate us but also awaken pangs which dissatisfy and corrupt. Love is an unstable passion, opening us both to the perfection of that for which it strives, and the sense of incompleteness of which such striving always makes us aware. The love of bodies, Plato tells us in the *Symposium*, leads us naturally to a love of the beautiful, then the good, and finally eternity itself. But, as every lover knows, addiction to the passion of love's continual self-overcoming, or some corrupting surrogate, can also usurp the divine gift of that end. Yet Plato also taught that this unrest and ambiguity lay at the heart of our existence: it was the creative tension which nourished the possibility of human excellence.

Grant taught us to love our own. To be immersed in our own is not yet to love our own, for that identity does not allow of the difference which sparks desire. But if love indicates to us a lack, and if by loving we express a dissatisfaction, how could our own be loved and yet also satisfy us by providing us a stable refuge from the tumult of powerfully transforming forces? If we are aware of our dissatisfaction, and of something different beyond our own, how could we love and respect our own ? But what, moreover, could there be beyond our own, which was not simply someone else's "own" ?

To these questions, there could be no simple answers. What Grant offered instead was a set of meditations, whose dominant symbols — technology, justice, politics, history, nature, our own, the good, God — were condensations of experiences which he took to belong essentially to our humanity. These meditations provided no simple solutions, held out for no rapid social transformations, and made no promises of systematic philosophic truth. Instead, they circled through the complex and ambiguous moments of our human condition — life and death, justice and injustice, knowledge and ignorance — portraying the unrest at the heart of our existence. Participating in and maintaining that condition of unrest, Grant understood from Plato, ensures decent regimes and spiritual nourishment. There could be no cessation of the darkness outside and within. To be human was to be receptive to the ambiguity of human existence. Dreams of perfect states of conciliation at the level of politics were not only unworldly, but anti-worldly; at the level of spirituality such dreams challenged to replace the distinctively human conflicts of virtue and vice by a tensionless, non-human existence. The human condition of darkness was an opportunity for prudent, political accommodation or philosophic and poetic symbolization, not speculative or activist manipulation. It was a condition which makes us *need* to be good, a condition which, with Plato, Grant could express as *love*.

By loving our own. That deceptively simple phrase opens us to complex reflections on our fate and the expectations we can reasonably hold as humans. As an experience which immediately invites to a meditative reflection on all its constituent moments, our "own," in Grant's writings, was always an origin and a terminus. The route beyond and back to our own was necessary and yet also dangerous. Circumnavigating the alluring modern shoals of corruption, deformation, surrogate satisfaction, and forgetfulness was both what threatened, and yet was the one thing vital to, the health of our nation. No work in Grant's writings fails to explore this tension nor its accompanying dangers.

This is nowhere so clear as in *Lament for a Nation*. Its publication in 1965 heralded the renewal among Canadians of an increasingly self-conscious desire to assess what was distinctive and worth cherishing in their legacy. In *Lament*, George Grant meditates on the difficult tension between particular Canadian loyalties and the lure of continental, economic expansion and how it has given us a privileged insight into the forces that constitute modern life. Canada is thus portrayed as a kind of "microcosm" of humanity's confrontation with the powerful, transformative forces of the West.

The upshot of Grant's assessment is contained in the term "lament." Canadians, on the one hand, were a people animated by their unique historical origins, their own particular land, their own founding myths, their own distinctive political symbols and self-interpretations. According to Grant, this meant a commitment to tory strains of respect for the community and nation, recognition of cultural practices that sustain orderly, political right, and diverse philanthropic strains of charity and duty based on the moral project of equality. Ours was a conservatism animated by a sense of the virtuous, bearing the hallmarks of prudence, prescription, reverence, order, and moderation. As such, it was also a communitarianism, based on the project of economic and social equality. What Grant recalled — against the empire-building of Macdonald and the Grand Alliance of 1854 — was the pre-modern substance of Canadian patriotism. This patriotism, unlike its simulacrum nationalism, evoked not merely an imaginary identity, but a tradition and a place — organizations of time and space constituting our unique British heritage. Being a Canadian had meant being grounded in these historical legacies.

On the other hand, Canadians have been lured by a Faustian dream of perpetual innovation and expansion, a dream made real in the vast technological development undertaken by the American empire. That empire proceeded as if its ideological project was simply rational and necessary. The Faustian process involved both endless alteration to the natural world and limitless change to the self engaged in the transformative process, all within what is taken to be a perfect system. The outcome, Grant predicted, could only be the loss of the stable contexts, prescriptive norms, and orienting experiences which had, in the past, provided for order and meaning in Canadian life, giving it moral vision. Grant lamented the passing of Canadian nationalism but with it, too, the end of a people's ability to resist what now threatened to engulf the established and familiar of the traditional world. What had been testimony to a spiritually more profound way of being human was now losing its public relevance. Moreover, it was the creative tension of existence itself that was being shut off by the assumption of the American empire to have made further historical action or philosophic/poetic work unnecessary.

Against this, no simple appeal to the past could be effective. Grant has often been called a "conservative," and in some senses of the word he may have been. But he also knew that embalming the virtues of the past was to condemn oneself to antiquarianism or romanticism, if not worse. There was no turning back; at best, we could think what we were doing — that is, experiencing the diremptions of the modern spiritual condition, thus purging ourselves of them and moderating our extravagant expectations of modern ideological fervour.

There were two thinkers who taught Grant to recognize the modern diremptions of the spirit — Leo Strauss and Martin Heidegger.

Strauss' importance shows clearly in light of how Grant came later to see his first book *Philosophy in the Mass Age* (1959). In that book, Grant had adopted the progressivism of Hegel and conceived the possibility of a modernity that embraced the best of the ancient and modern worlds — virtue and technology, rational order and freedom. The leisure afforded by technology, Grant believed, would allow for the regaining of those human purposes which had an eternal reference, celebrated by classical political philosophy. His hope was for a future society that would have within it "all that was good in the antique world and yet keep all the benefits of technology."[1]

Grant's disillusionment with modernity is registered initially in his comments on the Kojeve-Strauss debate regarding Strauss' interpretation of Xenophon's *Hiero*. He accepts the verdict that the universal and homogeneous state is a universal tyranny; more importantly, he rejects the terms of Kojeve's analysis by assuming, with Strauss, the prerogative to judge such a regime as unsatisfactory: he makes a superhistorical appeal to what humans are fitted for and, thus, to unchanging conceptions of human excellence. The pursuit of technological advance governing all contemporary doings was, in the end — accepting Strauss's verdict — a debasement of human excellence. Thus, "men being what they are," Grant wrote in his Introduction to the 1966 edition of *Philosophy in the Mass Age*,

> ...there are some who cannot find an adequate moral philosophy in the self-authenticating worship of technique and the liberalism which rationalizes it... Since the modern age has destroyed as living options all other traditions but itself, such people must turn back to the past in the hope of finding there what has been lost in the dynamic present.[2]

Leo Strauss would teach Grant that "on many of the most important political matters, Plato's teaching is truer than Hegel's."[3]

Like Strauss then, Grant begins his re-casting of the meaning of modernity by identifying this time as one of great uncertainty, as an "urgent present." This permits him to re-create a history of philosophic texts by which the decisive political questions can be asked. Like Strauss he is prudently reserved in drawing attention to those clashes of tradition — between reason and revelation, political order and virtue, citizenship and humanness — which might cause political disorder. Socratic irony, in the form of political prudence, leads both thinkers to recognize that defence of the rights tradition within liberalism is the appropriate stance from which to guarantee decency. (This was to be Grant's political persona, inspired by his favourite statement about politics: Thomas More's "When you can't make the good happen, prevent the very worst from happening.")

Persuaded by Strauss, Grant locates the source of the present crisis in the consequences of modernity's call for the conquest of fortune. As Strauss details in "Three Waves of Modernity," the cumulative effect of Machiavelli, Rousseau, and Nietzsche has been to destroy nature as a standard of anything other than what man should flee from; to elevate the possibility of a generalized will over the actuality of virtue; and to substitute the play of power, for reason's quest for the good, as the first cause of human striving. The search for the eternal — now only an "imaginary republic" (Machiavelli) — is abandoned; teleology in nature or providence is replaced by mechanical necessity and chance; and the primacy of the political regime and its distinctive virtues is overturned in favour of social forces and the motive of social recognition. With the progressive radicalization of the Machiavellian teaching, what *is*, becomes what man has *named*; what is named becomes arbitrary and accidental; and what is arbitrary and accidental must be mastered within a safe disciplinary matrix. This culminates in a radical historicism combined with the slavishness of the last man, which, with Nietzsche, one may call a condition of "nihilism" — a failure of spirit as well as the loss of all standards. But Nietzsche, through the obliteration of the tradition of political philosophy and all the categories by which it organized its teachings, takes us to a crossroads from which a new encounter or re-encounter with the ancients can proceed.

Strauss showed Grant the way in this history-of-an-error. With Strauss, Grant rejected historical progress and acknowledged that modern forces culminated in nihilism. But, unlike Strauss, Grant follows Jacques Ellul to see technology as an all-encompassing second reality. Behind this account stands Heidegger.

Especially in his later works, Grant follows Heidegger in focussing on the implications of the modern desire to fashion knowledge on the model of algebra. Thus, he accepts that technology comes to us as a complete ontological package,[4] and emphasizes the triumph of technology over every facet of our existence: in its transformative effect not only on the contents and context of our existence, but also on the categories of consciousness by which thought is organized into speech. Grant's own contribution is to examine what this has meant for individual freedom, for the diversity of being, and for the self's reverencing of the divine. As one measure of Grant's departure from Strauss, one should note the centrality in his analysis of the will — as the principle of our unique individuality, the source of our spontaneous free acts, and the origin of our concern with beginnings and nativity — and thus his greater concern for the ravages technology wreaks on human subjectivity.

So important to Grant's thought is this acceptance of Heidegger's assessment of technology that it is worthwhile to consider it at some length. Following Heidegger, Grant teaches us that we must view technology not just as an ensemble of machines, nor even simply as a mode of consciousness. It is rather a context, a condition which increasingly pervades our practices and skills, our self-interpretations and our desires. In the end, we are technology. Grant's work can be seen as a continued meditation on what Zdravko Planinc insightfully identified as the "spiritual condition that allows for the existence of technological society."

Technology, to use Heidegger's terms, is a way of being, or better, of revealing being, where man must "enframe" the world: a mechanized procuring in which man composes, rearranges, and orders the world. Here "man" is the "measure of all things," making himself, in Descartes' terms, "master and possessor of nature." As unified subject, as centre of all that is, he will serve his self-designated ideals, laying waste to whatever he designates as "other." What cannot be endowed with a determinate finitude, ordered on a grid table, or "operationalized" within his models and scenarios, is out of the order of things. The paradigmatic technological act is the act of appropriation by which reality is seized and made to utter its truth: the truth, as it has come to be understood, subsumes all the things and phenomena of the world as "objects." It is inseparable from the exercise of power.

It was Nietzsche who taught us that our century would understand its fate wholly within the dynamic activity of the "will-to-power." By this he meant that, whereas in the past we justified ourselves by appealing to nature, God, or history — as the contexts of our actions and speeches — now we realize that there is only the pure process of becoming. With the self-consciousness that accompanies Nietzsche's, and now our recognition that "God is dead" — that is, that all metaphysical foundations for our existence have dissolved — our desires, practices, and thoughts can be understood exclusively as active or reactive moments in the cyclical becoming of the will-to-power. Heidegger saw that the momentum of this will-to-power now resides in technology, a technology that is in essence expansionary. "Power," Nietzsche had explained, "exists only insofar as its power increases and insofar as [the will-to-power] commands this increase."[5] Thus, as Ellul suggests, technology is self-augmenting, self-justifying, and universalizing. Technology, as the will-to-power, does not take its bearings from any independent understanding of the true, the good, or the beautiful; it is its own justification.

This will-to-power, Grant recognized, will take the subtle form of a will-to-knowledge. This is the link between the will-to-power and technology. Our will-to-knowledge — our desire to know and master every facet of existence and to stockpile this information in vast data banks — makes it impossible to grasp truths independently of the technological act. Grant explored this in his essay, "Knowing and Making": as opposed to premodern receptivity to reality in the actionless and trusting consent to otherness, modern knowledge, beginning with Bacon and Descartes, must be a form of making, an experimental and suspicious appropriation of reality inspired by an enthusiasm for reconstructing the ambivalence and ambiguity of appearance. At the same time, "making," as well as all other doing, is henceforth guided by the procedural demands of scientific knowledge.[6] The independence of *theoria* as well as the Aristotelian distinction between *poesis* and *praxis* (making and action) is thereby relinquished. Reason becomes technical, regulative, and interventionist, rather than receptive. Repeated experimentation invites the suspicion that the instruments of making may constitute the objects they are intended to reveal. Further experimentation is required to test the instruments. The inquiry involves a questioning of the conditions of its own possibility, and invariably leads to the recognition that what is taken as "true" is built on conditions which are contingent, arbitrary, and adjustable. Every move towards apparently greater objectivity simply reconfirms the willful subjectivity and arbitrariness of the act. Reality or meaning is permitted to express itself only through relentless experimentation, but it is a reality which constantly eludes grasp. Oblivious to eternity, we have replaced receptivity to the transcendent with infinite and indefinite tasks of mastery — a nihilistic purposiveness without purpose. Such mastery has negated the ambiguities and mysteries of human existence as well as that creative tension which Plato saw as ensuring decent regimes and spiritual nourishment.

The impact of this condition, Grant argued, has been felt most strongly in the moral sphere. Whereas the Western tradition, has been sustained by a "justice in human relationships ... [that] was the essential way in which human beings are opened to eternity," Grant reminds us, the most extensive moral projects of the contemporary period are those which must ultimately subordinate justice to "human conveniences which fit the convenience of technology."[7] We can pay lip-service to "rights" and "justice" but these are understood as arbitrary and artificial constructs subordinate to the functions they perform, useful as formulaic protocols for serving some social purpose. They can thus be sacrificed for convenience or replaced with functional equivalents.

Our current efforts at moral speech, Grant claims, inevitably reproduce the logic of technology and cannot forestall the destructive effects of its nihilistic will-to-will. This is especially true of the projects that conceive of an "alternative" basis for our moral existence, projects whose language is that of "self," "creativity," "values," and "persons." This language celebrates man's free-will acts and his capacity to transform the very nature of valuation itself. "Morality," Grant reminds us, "is above all concerned with the frontiers and limitations of making," but when those limits are defined by our will, everything can be rendered conditional and disposable.[8] We cannot equate "willing" with moral guidance, since the unconditional end towards which we are guided is excluded by the act of will. Rather than receiving purpose or condition, will defines them. Even the "Kantians," who obviously recognize the centrality of morality, are just "great delayers," as Nietzsche called them, for they cannot put off the destiny of their unstable language, as "such destinies have a way of working themselves out — that is, of bringing forth from their principle everything which is implied in that principle."[9]

The perplexity surrounding moral limits manifests itself clearly in two of our most extreme technological interventions: abortion and euthanasia. Focusing primarily on the euphemisms — "quality of life," "right to reproductive freedom," "mercy killing," "benign neglect" — that obscure the nature of these acts, Grant reminds us that the integrity of what we recognize as "justice" is measured by how we treat our weakest social members. In the interests of the strong, and by virtue of the will-to-power which now motivates us, any understanding of the rights of the unborn and of the disabled as self-evident has been largely extinguished. What we have instead are contrivances of control which pass for the satisfaction of our moral obligations. When "quality of life" and "personhood" become administered simply by virtue of a definition, or as a result of a means-test, the question is whether we are still dealing with human beings in their particular, concrete existence. While these methodic procedures of contemporary justice-administration are efficient, and while they achieve the long-term goals of prosperity and public health, Grant wonders whether there are features of being human which are foreclosed, experiences that sanction our confidence in saying what is "due" or "proper" to human life.

It is here that Grant departs most decisively from both Strauss and Heidegger. While appearing to flirt with a radical historicism precluding a restoration of classical thought, and thus justifying Dennis Lee's suggestion that Grant was at an impasse, Grant is not silent before the technological dynamo. Acknowledging the difficulty that the language of unconditional limits has in the public world, Grant nonetheless affirms that even within the regime of modern technology, we receive an "apprehension of the world beyond that as a field of objects considered as pragmata"[10] and experience "intimations of essential deprivals"[11] which ultimately open us up to "the core of what has been handed over to us from Athens and Jerusalem is this language of good and evil, and that it is a language which belongs to man as man."[12] Indeed, such experiences lie at the heart of his strong and unconditional moral stance on abortion and euthanasia. This stance, while expressed in the idiom of modern-rights teaching, harkens back to a pre-modern respect for the sacredness of life. At the level of concepts and ideas, whose intelligibility is vouchsafed by public authority and social legitimacy, we are at what Lee has called "Grant's impasse." But at the experiential level, we are always capable of the meditative enactment of those spiritual experiences given to us as human beings.

An assessment of Grant's understanding of how we are to love our own, and to be sufficiently attentive to the tensions within it, requires thinking about what Grant meant when he identified himself as a "political philosopher within Christianity."[13] This requires recognizing that, for Grant, the most complete life involves not only thinking, but also remembering and loving, activities which proclaim philosophy at work in the world composing a moral community. Morality, for Grant, is seen not as an alternative to, or the political face of, the philosophic life, but as its condition of possibility. Barry Cooper elegantly explains what this meant for Grant: "Political philosophy is within Christianity as the line is within the circle, as our erotic search for perfection is within the completeness of the whole." There is a comprehensiveness to Christianity — in its demand upon us to think time and eternity, self and soul, and wisdom and free will together — which, for Grant, completes ancient wisdom.

Joan O'Donovan explains that this required reconfirming our apprehension of ourselves as finite beings capable of participating in the divine perfection, and the further apprehension of the teleology of all created, finite beings, which undergirds our sense of cosmological order and supplies us with an awareness of the proper limits to our actions. She notes that beyond the bargains and conveniences of our project to master human and non-human nature, it is given to us to participate in God's providential order of created goods. While under the conditions of human sin, it is an apprehension which sees the whole as a unity of law and love. From this position, what Grant has to say about technology requires us to think about and reunite the meaning of created order and the cross of Christ, for our error is to have "absorbed the meaning of both created being and saving being into the technological possibilities of matter for us." Opposition to the loveless totality of technology — its purposelessness and "sempereternity of the same" means recovering the "consent to the fact [of] authentic otherness."[14] Such consent underlies Grant's understanding of faith. "Faith," Grant writes, "is the experience that intelligence is enlightened by love."[15] The task for a "political philosopher within Christianity" is to think together the law of love and the rule of law without being drawn into either rigid doctrinairism on the one hand, or the charm of ineffability or transcendent mystery on the other. Grant's moderation concerning both temptations is expressed in his recognition that:

> ...Western Christianity simplified the divine love by identifying it too closely with immanent power in the world... . Both Protestants and Catholics became triumphalist by failing to recognise the distance between the order of good and the order of necessity... [Yet] the web of necessity which the modern paradigm of knowledge lays before us does not tell us that God is dead, but reminds us of what western Christianity seemed to forget in its moment of pride: how powerful is the necessity which love must cross. Christianity did not produce its own gravedigger, but the means to its own purification.[16]

And that purification entails, as Joan O'Donovan suggests, the recovery of the rational "language of what belongs to man as man."

However that might occur — and obviously such a recovery would be immensely difficult — Grant does leave us with a set of meditations by which the philosophical work can begin. These meditations have no simple ideological message. Instead, they serve to remind us of the inevitable uncertainties of our existence and of our difficult "in-between" nature as the being that experiences finiteness and creatureliness, but that also is dissatisfied with a state experienced as imperfect. "Justice" was the symbol for Grant of the spiritual condition in which this unrest was fully experienced. And "justice," as it demands of us to love our own as the necessary prelude to any human excellence, and as it requires of us to live with the uncertainty and ambiguity of our human existence, was Grant's abiding theoretical and practical concern. In a wish to pay tribute to that life's work, the conference "George Grant and the Legacy of Lament for a Nation" was held September 22-24, 1989 in Ottawa at Carleton University.

The papers that follow arise from that event commemorating the enduring achievement of George Grant. They are organized according to the four major themes in Grant's work: the political independence of Canada, the revival of political philosophy, the continued significance of a religious life, and the relation between technology and justice.

We attempted, at the conference, to combine the formal, structured nature of conference papers with the *psuchagogia* and erotic nature of conversation. I subsequently asked the moderators of the discussions to summarize the essence of those conversations. While these summaries cannot convey the enthusiasm of erotic soul-leading, nor display the structured precision of philosophic analysis, they do set out a terrain of questions and issues which we thought it would be profitable to include in this collection.

Grant dedicated the work which constitutes the epitome of his writings, *English-Speaking Justice*, to Alex Colville and Dennis Lee. Each has held up a mirror that reflects not only our condition in the here-and-now, but also our place in a larger whole. Colville has portrayed the sterility and ennui of contemporary life against the sublimity and power of the natural world. The directness and immediacy of his paintings at once link the viewer with the concreteness of everyday life and separate him from it. From geometrical principles Colville achieves an almost mystical or religious effect — indeed, this is why Grant could say of "Truck Stop" that he and his son could contemplate the painting in silent rapport. Reflecting on the importance of geometry for order, one is reminded of the education of the guardians in Plato's *Republic*, where mathematics is called upon to temper the soul and provide it with reasoned measure, as the prelude to reasoned speech.

Education in mathematics, however, must be supplemented by education in music, Plato teaches, if the soul is not to become inflexible and irascible. Dennis Lee's magnificent meditation on Grant as a witness to the impasse of the modern condition — the inability to hold classical and modern truth in unity — speaks to our spiritual longings, our desire for transcendence, our erotic impulse towards the good, our yearnings for a justice animated by the fire of love. His haunting sense of our predicament stems from a passion which is properly a poet's — one who writes of the whole.

I would like to speculate that Grant understood Plato's point that the philosophers' reflections on justice are like the weaving together of distinct strands of materials that may not even have a natural affinity for one another. Justice comprises the steadfastness of mathematical order and the erotic mania of poetic inspiration. For Plato and, I believe, Grant, such weaving constituted the supreme art of statesmanship. I like to think that Grant's dedication of *English-Speaking Justice* to Colville and Lee brings together mathematics and poetry. It is as much an act of justice as an account of justice. Because Grant expressed his friendship with Colville and Lee in such a manner, it seemed appropriate to have them lead off our volume. Moreover, in an environment inhospitable to philosophy's task, it now increasingly falls to artists and poets to proclaim publicly the tensions and unrest, the enraptured experiences and intimations of deprival, that comprise the human condition.

Grant knew they could only do so mythically. Our desire to see the language and experience of the good manifest as measures in our political and spiritual world, and as the product of philosophical analysis, could only be an ambivalent yearning. This is what makes

Colville's portrait of Grant, the howling wolf depicted on the Canadian fifty-cent piece, so apt. For, as Farley Mowat at the end of *Never Cry Wolf* depicts, in his poignant comment on how Canadians understand their fate, the howling wolf conveys for us the painful ambivalence of time, and our longings for a world from which time has now distanced us:

> Somewhere to the eastward a wolf howled; lightly, questioningly. I knew the voice, for I had heard it many times before. It was George, sounding the wasteland for an echo from the missing members of his family. But for me it was a voice which spoke of the lost world which once was ours before we chose the alien role; a world which I had glimpsed and almost entered... only to be excluded, at the end, by my own self.[17]

The same ambivalent yearning underlies Lee's charming poem "The Wizard and the Cat" — on coming to love the good by first loving our own; the ferocious tornness of "The Gods"; and the poems of ending and beginning, leaving and coming home, from "Nightwatch." In each case too, we are brought to lament the forgetting of the good once present in our love of our own and of the creative tensions which ensured moderation and common sense, still understandable as the great guarantors of public decency.

Mel Hurtig is the nationalist of whom we first think when we recall Grant's political teaching; we recall his unflagging and spirited defence of our own, and his hopeful vision of a future economic and cultural independence. David Warren, editor of that paragon of southern Ontario culture, *The Idler*, speaks from the deepest core of one of Canada's founding myths — the loyalist tradition — to draw us anamnetically to our British origin. The panellists — Gad Horowitz, Andy Stark, Don Forbes, Kim Campbell, Rainer Knopff, and Janet Ajzenstat — adjudicate the tension between them. Barry Cooper explains Grant's understanding of the importance of the revival of political philosophy, reminding us that Grant's is not an immediately practical warning, but a point of departure for reflections about the situation in the modern world. Michael Gillespie sums up a rich discussion by Clifford Orwin, Howard Brotz, William Mathie, Wayne Whillier, and Randy Newell by focusing on the significance of Heidegger to those who would take political responsibility seriously. Joan O'Donovan considers the place of the natural-law teaching in Grant's reflections on human justice, and the implications of our current groundlessness. Subsequent discussion by Randall Marlin, Tim Fuller, John Robertson, and John Dourley is summarized by Louis Greenspan and John Kirby. Ken Minogue challenges Grant on the issue of technology and its impact on our understanding of justice. He is answered by Ed Andrew and Zdravko Planinc in their summary of the engaging debates between Peter Self, Tom Darby, and James Wiser. Bill Christian, quoting Grant, sums up what each of us perhaps tried to say of Grant's enduring significance:

> About the magic of art in which the dance of this prodigality is achieved — well, it is magic, and I cannot speak of it here and perhaps not at all.

There is neither profound disagreement nor profound agreement among the writers. Yet if, out of so many disparate viewpoints and positions, we can draw one common lesson, it is that our condition does not permit of the final word or solution. It is part of the human condition that our interpretive efforts and our political interventions remain imperfect and incomplete. The lesson of moderation is not a dismal one. The darkness both outside and within is escaped, by dreams, only at our peril.

NOTES

1   George Grant, *Philosophy in the Mass Age*. (Toronto: Copp Clark Publishing, 1959), p. vii.

2   Ibid., p. v.

3   George Grant, "Introduction," *Philosophy in the Mass Age*. (Toronto: Copp Clark, 1966), p. viii.

4   George Grant, "Thinking About Technology," *Technology and Justice*. (Toronto: Anansi Press, 1986), p. 32.

5   Quoted in Martin Heidegger, *Nietzsche: The Will to Power as Art*, vol.1 (New York: Harper and Row, 1979), p. 267.

6   George Grant, "Knowing and Making," *Transactions of the Royal Society of Canada*, 4th series, 1975, 12:59-67.

7   George Grant, *English-Speaking Justice*. (Sackville, New Brunswick: Mount Allison University, 1974), p. 90-91.

8   Grant, "Knowing and Making," op. cit. *supra*, p. 65.

9   *Ibid.*, p. 67.

10   Grant, "In Defence of North America," *Technology and Empire: Perspectives on North America*, (Toronto: House of Anansi Press Limited, 1969), p. 35.

11   George Grant, "A Platitude," *Technology and Empire: Perspectives on North America*. (Toronto: Anansi, 1969), p. 141.

12   George Grant, "Revolution and Tradition," *Canadian Forum*, 50:86.

13   George Grant, "Nietzsche and the Ancients," *Technology and Justice* (Toronto: House of Anansi Press, 1986), p. 92.

14   George Grant, "Faith and the Multiversity," *Technology and Justice*. (Toronto: House of Anansi Press, 1986), p. 38.

15   Ibid.

16   Ibid., p. 76-77.

17   Farley Mowat, *Never Cry Wolf*. (Toronto: McClelland and Stewart, 1963), p. 246.

PART I

INTRODUCTION

A TRIBUTE TO PROFESSOR GEORGE P. GRANT

Alex Colville

I am honoured to be taking part in this commemoration. I am not, of course, a philosopher or a political scientist, but philosophy has a kind of fascination for me, and I take politics very seriously—possibly more so than some political scientists. I think there are more connections than current society acknowledges between academe, the realm of abstract thought, and the arts, which are, in a sense, the realm of action, at least the realm of ideated action — I think of Bernard Berenson's wonderful phrase, "ideated sensation." As I think we all know, George Grant took some satisfaction from the knowledge that his work spilled over, so to speak, from the vessel of learned discourse into the public street. So I am an example of a person whose life and work have been influenced, or I might better say confirmed, by his thought.

Before going any further, I want to make clear that I was not an intimate friend of George Grant's; I cannot, and do not, claim extensive knowledge of him. In fact, he is something of a mystery to me. I shall refer to him as "George" for the sake of brevity (and because I called him that in life), but I do not want to seem presumptuous or overly familiar; he was a dignified person.

I first met him at a seminar organized by McMaster University, held at an Anglican retreat in Dundas, Ontario, in July 1963. In the roughly two dozen of us gathered there, many disciplines were represented; among those attending were Iris Murdoch, then still teaching, and her husband John Bayley of New College, Oxford. We spent a week in wide-ranging discussion. George's contribution was memorable; certainly his character made a lasting impression on me. One might ask why this was so.

I had decided, in February 1963 (February is a month of trauma in universities) that I could not stay in a university because I found some of my colleagues literally intolerable. (By this time George had resigned from two universities.) My point is that I found satisfaction at this McMaster colloquium. I suppose if I were to state simply my rather child-like reaction to George Grant it would be this: Here is a real professor. I want to consider, a little later, the effect of such a professor on students.

What did George say? What I have in my memory is a kind of *gestalt* — what has been defined as "a symbolic configuration having properties that cannot be derived from its parts." When I try to pull elements out of the *gestalt* of his talk and writings, I think of his concern that in our society, few people were acting like thinking men — that there was no bridge between actual government and moral philosophy; or, to put it in more fundamental and more positive terms, that people should be *thinking about how to be good*. If I may speak about my own work as a painter, I have been for many years, many decades, interested in the concept of creatures who, while living, are thinking about life. Implicit in this is the conviction that thought, and the action resulting from thought, may be good or bad. Persons are living in history, in the specific here and now, while attempting to be congruent with some transcending essence beyond history. This may result, oddly, in a kind of shifting between "angst" and tranquillity. Although my friend and early patron Lincoln Kirstein told me that I painted two-legged and four-legged animals, my representations of animals are of innocent being, innocent action, and so are exemplary. Human creatures are often represented as contemplating the life that goes on around them. (Milan Kundera has said that a poet is a person whose mother has made him display himself before a world he cannot enter.) I mention all this because George embodied the idea of a man thinking about how one might be good in the present and actual world. And so my representations were justified — *quod erat demonstrandum*. Thus George was for me a kind of proof.

I shared with him the conviction that much of what passed for art, for culture, in our era was a kind of degenerate play, whose function it was to divert people's attention from serious things. Not only should there be a bridge between moral philosophy and action (in Hannah Arendt's sense of action), but there should also be a connec-

4

tion, delicate and difficult, between aesthetics and moral philosophy. I hesitate to quote George to people who have read him more deeply and more extensively than I have, but I must quote him here: "The public purpose of art will not be to lead men to the meaning of things, but to titivate, cajole and shock them into fitting into a world in which the question of meaning is not relevant [emphasis mine[1]].

Because we were nearly contemporaries (born 1918 and 1920), George and I shared an interest in French existentialism, available to me only in translation. We had both been gravely affected by the second World War and the questions of conduct that were raised by the Nazi phenomenon and the holocaust. (The question in my mind at the end of the war was, What does this mean?) There were questions not only of what to think, but of what to do. George, like the American poet Robert Lowell (both of them aristocrats) was a conscientious objector — a path more difficult, and in George's case I think more dangerous, than the conventional one I followed. We had both been moved, for want of a better word, by the writings of Simone Weil. I remember once saying to George that, just as Sartre, Camus, Simone de Beauvoir (and Iris Murdoch) had turned from philosophy to fiction in order to make ideas work, so to speak, so he had fixed on the person and career of Diefenbaker in order to embody almost literally, his concepts of moral philosophy. We said that we would talk about this more later, but we never did. I do think his *Lament for a Nation* introduced a wider public to his thought; as Dean Acheson said when asked why he was a democrat, "All conservatives are not stupid, but all stupid people are conservative."

It is worth speculating about the extent to which George's concepts were transmitted to leading figures in Canadian government. I remember being at a conference on Canadian culture in 1964 in St. Adele, Quebec. At that time culture came under the office of the Secretary of State, who was the late Maurice Lamontagne, a Harvard-educated economist and an intelligent, attractive and sensitive man. He spoke to us workers in the arts about his judgement of the value of what we were doing, and in such a way that he received a standing ovation from us — something I have seen only once in my life. I was impressed by Lamontagne; at a gathering before dinner I asked him if he knew George Grant's writing. He did not. I thought: I am old enough that I shouldn't be disappointed. But how sad that George's work, with its sympathy for French culture in general and for Quebec's peculiar plight in particular, should be virtually unknown in that province.

We also shared a sense of being distinctly North American. I am the son of an immigrant from lowland Scotland who became a structural steel worker (my father's birth certificate describes his father's occupation as "carter"). I find these lines from "In Defence of North America" both extremely funny and absolutely true: "To the Europeans also we appear as spawned by themselves; the children of some low class servants who once dared to leave the household and who now surprisingly appear as powerful and dominating neighbours masquerading as gentry, whose threat can only be minimized by teaching them a little culture."[2] Both as a painter and as a person I see myself as one whose life and work involve issues, and take place in contexts, which no European (and more obviously no Asian) has experienced. At the same time I acknowledge, as I think George did, my enormous debt to certain Europeans (and Egyptians) of very long ago — and thus my lack of "originality." So one looks for navigational principles inherited from the Mediterranean in order to find a course in our more remote and perhaps less sheltering waters — which would have to include Mark Twain's Mississippi, as well as Captain Joshua Slocum's Bay of Fundy.

Our relationship was to some degree reciprocal, and I think George's interest in my work arose partly out of his sensing that my use of geometry (sometimes described as obsessive) was like the ancient Greek (non-utilitarian and, therefore, in some sense religious) concept of a kind of government of mathematics which operated in space in the visual arts and in time in dance, music, and poetry. It is interesting that George's quality of openness, of undulled receptivity, allowed him to apprehend this, while he claimed to have no real understanding, at least no detailed specific understanding, of the place of mathematics in aesthetics.

I referred earlier to Professor Grant's influence as a teacher; I use the title "professor" as a form of homage. (I would like to see people who teach in universities referred to as Mr., Miss, Ms.; the most significant would be called Professor. If one wants to know the academic degrees held by someone, this can be found in the calendar.)

The 50-cent coin design.
(© Alex Colville 1990/.VIS*ART Copyright Inc.)

I have known several people whose lives were, I can only say, changed by George. In the past, thinking of my own children, I have thought what a blessing it is that the young, including university students, pay so little attention to their teachers that the influence of bad teachers seems to be negligible. By a bad teacher I do not mean someone deficient in pedagogical technique. I mean stupid people and evil people; the latter may be intelligent, and may include psychopaths. So the young develop a kind of armour, but this may also cut them off from those comparatively rare teachers who, as I believe was said of Francis of Assisi, "want them to be."

I think that the sense among some students of being deprived while standing amidst plenty opened them up to George, who was open. Sometime in the seventies I gave a slide lecture on my work at McMaster; I was surprised and delighted to see George and his wife in the audience. He listened, and presumably looked, in the way that a few good students do, in that open and vulnerable way. (When Camus first came to New York after the second World War an acute observer said his essential characteristic was vulnerability.) I think George's students realized that he was learning and learning from them, while teaching.

The day I first met George I noticed that he had specks of white paint on his brown shoes, presumably from house-painting. I thought: An unworldly guy. He was at that time a passionate smoker. He told me that one of his sisters told him that he was killing himself smoking; he told me this hurt his feelings. In a discussion at McMaster, after he had made a somewhat Nietzschean statement, I said to him I thought his remark was romantic — he told me that I had hurt his feelings. This tenderness in him I always thought admirable; we have enough tough guys.

I will close with two anecdotes. First, when I designed and made the models for the Canadian centennial coins I could not find any persons admirable enough to be commemorated (no Jefferson, General Grant, or Roosevelt) so I used (commemorated) six animals. For the fifty-cent piece I made an image of a howling wolf. I sent one to George; I told him it was a portrait of him.

Second, in 1966 I painted "Truck Stop." Because my friend, the late T.R. MacDonald, was then the director of the Hamilton Art Gallery

Truck Stop, Collection Ludwig Museum, Cologne,
(© Alex Colville 1990/VIS*ART Copyright Inc.)

I first exhibited the painting in that gallery. George wrote me something that moved me — perhaps the most complimentary remark ever made to me about my work. The painting shows the central part of a Mack cab-over-engine eighteen-wheel truck at an Esso station in the early morning (other people call it evening). The pump attendant has a broken arm in a cast in a sling. A German shepherd dog is smelling one of the tires of the truck. George wrote me that this painting was something he and his fourteen-year-old son could contemplate in silent rapport.

NOTES

1   George Grant, *Technology and Empire — Perspectives on North America* (Toronto: House of Anansi Press, 1969), p.127.

2   Ibid., p.16.

GRANT'S IMPASSE

Dennis Lee

I

I'd like to start with a poem which, for me, has a particular association that makes it appropriate for a conference on George Grant's thought. Let me explain.

George Grant once gave me a particular gift. We were sitting in the living room of his house in Dundas. I'd been telling him about the patch of ground where I most belong — a couple of acres by a lake north of Toronto, where we spent the summers when I was a boy.

"How *marvellous*, Dennis!" he boomed, with that outsize gusto which always took me off guard. A tumble of ashes came snaking down his cardigan. "How *marvellous*! It's what Plato meant, isn't it?..." Abruptly I felt myself paddling along about twenty steps behind him. How had Plato come into this?

But on he went — more gingerly, I thought. " ...That we're made to love the Good." W*hat*? I tried to interpret the shift in his tone, since the sense was eluding me. He seemed concerned that he might be offending me; evidently the connection between my cottage and the Good was so obvious that I might feel patronized if he spelled it out. I tried not to let my bewilderment show. "And the way we come to love the Good is by first loving our own.... How marvellous for you, having that place in Muskoka to love!" More ashes tumbled onto the cardigan.

By first loving our own! I still remember the little click with which that phrase slid into place, and I realised I actually knew what he was talking about. Grant was giving me back my instinctive, closer-than-breathing love for those pines, that rocky shoreline, the ram-shackle cottage: giving it back to me in a luminous further dimension.

George and Sheila Grant,
(used with the kind permission of William Christian.)

For cherishing this childhood place—that was not just something I did by accident. It was what I was fitted for. Humans are being human when they love their own. I'd always known that. And at the same time, loving the cottage was a necessary first step, something to grow ahead from — it schooled me to love less immediate forms of "the good." Yes, that too... Feeling so linked to that boyhood place of the heart, I'd known these things in a deep, pre-verbal way. I just never knew I knew them. Not until I heard them spoken out loud, in George and Sheila's living room.

Grant was also giving me, perhaps for the first time, Plato and the ancients. With those few throwaway remarks, I discovered more about the immediacy of classical thought than I had in several years of philosophy at the University of Toronto. For this wasn't some abstract, textbook theory; it knew my life more intimately than I did myself.

It's by way of thanks for that gift that I'd like to read you "The Cat and the Wizard." The poem is not an allegory; it's about a wizard and a cat. But I can see also that it concerns love of our here and now, which the cat knows especially; and love of our higher and deeper destinations, which is the wizard's calling. The rest of this paper will examine Grant's reluctant conclusion, that those two loves cannot be held together in thought in our era. But let me start with this tale, which declares what he equally knew: the two are inseparable, even when our minds can no longer think their unity.

THE CAT AND THE WIZARD

I

A senior wizard
of high degree
With a special diploma
In wizardry
Is trudging along
At the top of the street
With a scowl on his face
And a pain in his feet.

A beard, a bundle,
A right angle stoop,
And a cutaway coat
Embroidered with soup,
A halo of smoke
And a sputtery sound —
the only real magic
Magician around.

> But nobody nowadays
> Welcomes a wizard:
> They'll take in a spaniel,
> Make room for a lizard —
> But show them a conjurer
> Still on the ball,
> And nobody wants him
> Or needs him at all.

His bundle is bulging
With rabbits and string,
And a sort of machine
That he's teaching to sing,
And a clock, and a monkey
That stands on its head,
And a mixture for turning
Pure gold into lead.

He carries a bird's nest
That came from the Ark;
He knows how to tickle
A fish in the dark;
He can count up by tens
To a million and three —
But he can't find a home
For his wizardry.

> For *nobody*, nowadays,
> Welcomes a wizard;
> They'll drool at a goldfish,
> Repaint for a lizard,
> But show them a magus
> Who knows his stuff —
> They can't slam their latches down
> Quickly enough!

II

In Casa Loma
Lives a cat
With a jet-black coat
And a tall silk hat.
And every day
At half past four
She sets the table
For twelve or more.

The spoons parade
Beside each plate;
She pours the wine,
She serves the steak,
And Shreddies, and turnips,
And beer in a dish —
Though all she can stomach
Is cold tuna fish.

> But a cat is a cat
> In a castle or no,
> And people are people
> Wherever you go.

Then she paces about
In the big dining hall,
Waiting and waiting
For someone to call
Who won't be too snooty
For dinner and chat
At the home of a highly
Hospitable cat.

And every evening
At half past eight,
She throws out the dinner
And locks the gate.
And every night,
At half past ten,
She climbs up to bed
By herself, again.

> For a cat is a cat
> In a castle or no,
> And people are people
> Wherever you go.

III

One day they meet
In a laundromat,
The lonesome wizard,
The coal-black cat.

And chatting away
In the clammy air,
They find they both like
Solitaire,

And merry-go-rounds,
And candle-light,
And spooky yarns
That turn out right.

They stroll together
Chatting still
To Casa Loma
On the hill

And there the cat
Invites her friend
To share a bite,
If he'll condescend;

And yes, the wizard
Thinks he might —
But just for a jiffy
And one quick bite.

An hour goes by
Like a silver skate.
The wizard moves
From plate to plate.

Two hours go by,
Like shooting stars.
The cat produces
Big cigars

And there in the darkening
Room they sit,
A cat and a wizard,
Candle-lit.

At last the wizard
Takes the pack
From his creaking, reeking,
Rickety back.

He sets it down
With a little shrug,
And pulls a rabbit
From under the rug.

And before you can blink
He's clapping his hands
And there in the doorway
A peacock stands!

Now he's setting the monkey
Upon its head,
He's turning the silverware
Into lead,

And counting by tens
From a hundred to four
And making a waterfall
Start from the floor

And juggling a turnip,
A plate and a dish,
And turning them all
Into fresh tuna fish.

The cat is ecstatic!
She chortles, she sails
From the roof to the floor
On the banister rails,

And soon the whole castle
Is whizzing with things:
With sparklers and flautists
And butterflies' wings,

And all through the night
The party goes on —
Till it stops in a trice
At the crack of dawn,

And the wizard installs
His pack in a drawer,
While the cat tidies up
The living-room floor.

And as the sky
Is growing red,
They tiptoe up
The stairs to bed.

The wizard's snore
Is rather weird;
The cat is snuggled
In his beard —

Dreaming of tuna fish
End to end,
And rabbits, and having
A brand-new friend.

Perhaps you wonder
How I know
A cat and a wizard
Can carry on so?

Well: if some day
you chance to light
On Casa Loma
Late at night,

Go up to the window,
Peek inside,
And then you'll see
I haven't lied.

For round and round
The rabbits dance,
The moon is high
And they don't wear pants;

The tuna fish
Patrol the hall,
The butterflies swim
in the waterfall,

And high and low
With a hullaballoo
The castle whirls
Like a tipsy zoo.

And in the corner,
If you peer,
Two other figures
May appear.

One is dressed
In a tall silk hat:
The queen of the castle,
The jet black cat.

The other's a wizard
Of high degree.
The wizard is grinning
The wizard is me.

II

One year after his death, many of us carry a debt of love to George Grant. Honouring it this weekend can have nothing to do with sentimentalizing George or his thought. But that debt of love makes the words we mean to speak feel exposed, as though there were winds blowing through from space, or eternity.

Yet the exposure is also a shelter. For we need those winds; they're home.

They make me want to say bare things.

*

Grant wrote often of the need for holding classical truth and modern truth in the same thought. The good and technology; sacramental meaning and the fact/value distinction; natural law and freedom to invent the world; reverence and mastery. And for years I thought this was the programme he himself was trying to accomplish

— to think the unity of ancient and modern, to find rational categories that would let them stand as commensurable.

But that was wrong. Grant coveted such a reconciliation, but he didn't publish a single word that attempted to achieve it. In his written work, at least, his calling was different.

*

George Grant was a witness. His primary vocation in writing was to suffer with all his mind, and all his body, heart and soul, the emergence of the nihilism which had been unfolding over the past centuries from within the project of modernity. This nihilism stemmed from the increasing difficulty of discerning any sense in which we are subject to the claim of the good; indeed, any sense in which "claim" or "good" have substantial meaning at all. It fell to Grant to give witness to this civilisational end-game.

As well, his vocation was to articulate — for the first time ever, I believe — a short but crucial advance in the unfolding of that nihilism (which we'll come to shortly). Finally, his calling was to dwell nobly in the muteness of mind which he had uncovered, while cleaving to older truths in memory and desire, and living the best practical life he could.

That's not a vocation any sane person would choose: to bear witness to the closing down of articulate meaning in one's civilisation. But the vocation chose George Grant. Reckoning with his work means reading it in that light.

*

From this perspective, Grant's pivotal thinking was accomplished between 1967 and 1969. It is found in the essays of Technology and Empire. They constitute his most enduring achievement, I believe, even though in certain respects they're anomalous in his thought. I want to look at those extraordinary meditations now, that exceptional season of two or three years in his lifework.

In doing so, it's a temptation to over-explicate things which Grant has already said magnificently. Suffice it to say that I refer to the liberal paradigm which Leo Strauss had clarified for him: the model of an objective and value-free world, populated by free, calculating, and value-imputing subjects. And I'm pointing to the "oblivion of eternity" (Strauss' phrase) and the latent nihilism which were inseparable from the liberal split of the world into facts and values. That nihilism had taken several centuries to work to the surface; finally it had become apparent that, in objectifying the world to free us of superstition, and in relativising all values, liberalism had — along with its many heroic benefits — not only sent us out to spiritual starvation in a world of facts; it had left us no defence against even the most monstrous forms of tyranny. The prophet of this maturation of nihilism, for Grant, was Nietzsche.

Strauss saw certain things very clearly. When goodness, justice, truth and the rest of their now-spectral kin are denied any participation in a sacral and claiming order, indeed are denied any reality at all beyond that of historically-conditioned accident, there is no restraint we can plausibly invoke against the grossest acts of inhumanity. What obligation does anyone have to practise justice, when such a notion is merely one among many folkloric "values" — which arise amongst the natives in all times and places, but which can have no binding purchase upon us now, being themselves (paradoxically) no more than value-free objects of study? There is finally nothing in the liberal account of things that can tell us why Mother Teresa might be "better" than Hitler.

What liberalism comes to, then, is a batch of neuter facts, and the will to power. Anything more is sentimentality.

It is this impotence towards the reality of anything not the object of our own control which is named in the term "nihilism." And such an analysis situates the phenomenon, not in the moody negativity of individual temperaments, but in the processes which have powered liberal civilisation for centuries. Structural nihilism is not just a private stance we can choose to adopt or reject. It is now woven into our history and institutions and daily assumptions; it's a concrete, impersonal milieu into which we're born and which we inhabit.

*

Grant took over Strauss' anatomy of the nihilism of modern thought. And in *Technology and Empire* he put it on a still broader basis, by thinking through technology, imperialism, and the doctrine of radical freedom within its matrix. In the liberal world, all nature becomes raw material; and nature includes not only trees and lakes but other peoples, our own bodies, even the so-called "values." Everything is there to be processed by our radically free wills, using instrumental reason and technique. Eventually, in fact, we don't just use technique; we are it. Technique expresses our fundamental way of being in the world; it is our ontology, and by its very nature it excludes all modes of being but itself.

In the process, Grant rose to an eros of intellectual contemplation, a terrible passion in which the fate of the planet achieved some of its true contemporary names. His account folds into itself in profound simplicity, tracing the strange loops of our "unified fate" with vertiginous clarity. You all know those great elegiac passages; let me recall just one here, the conclusion of "In Defence of North America." Listen to how the symphonic cadences of witnessing lengthen our attention, slow down our agitated response, to the point where we are able to gaze into hard and terrible truths without just running out and *doing* something, anything, to make them disappear. For in the end we could only apply some new technique, blindly re-enacting the very condition that Grant is striving to bring to articulacy.

> ... as our liberal horizons fade in the winter of nihilism, and as the dominating amongst us see themselves with no horizon except their own creating of the world, the pure will to technology (whether personal or public) more and more gives sole content to that creating.... Within the practical liberalism of our past, techniques could be set within some context other than themselves — even if that context was shallow. We now move towards the position where technological progress becomes itself the sole context within which all that is other to it must attempt to be present.[1]

*

At this point in his thinking, Grant had tracked the nihilism of modern civilization further than Nietzsche had — not because he was a greater thinker, but because that nihilism had been in the ascendant a hundred years longer, and its practical results were far more advanced. And he had unravelled its contemporary workings more fully than either of his immediate mentors, Strauss or Jacques Ellul. Yet in a sense, Grant was still unpacking Nietzsche.

He now took a further step, which as far as I can tell — and I can hear George snorting in derision at the claim — constitutes an original contribution, and a decisive one, to the philosophic unfolding of our era. It seems a bit weak-kneed to add that it uncovers yet one more level of grue in technological society.

The step was this. Strauss had assailed modernity as though he himself had access to more-than-modern truths: namely, those of the classical philosophy whose restoration he urged. But in fact, Grant concluded in 1964 (in "Tyranny and Wisdom"), Strauss had not demonstrated how to articulate the truths of Athens or Jerusalem concretely — without transforming them to fit the modern mindset, which would by definition unselve them.

In arguing that Strauss had claimed a contemporary cogency for ancient truths which he was unable to make good in concrete thought, Grant was not rejecting the claim of those ancient truths. On the contrary: he insisted, rarely but then very firmly, that he himself had been absolutely claimed by them. He was a Christian, and a Platonist. But he parted company with Strauss over whether that being-claimed could be coherently articulated, or thought, or (sometimes) even entertained in a more-than-vestigial way, by anyone shaped by the civilisation we belong to.

There was the one burning example of Simone Weil, suggesting to Grant that it was possible. Yet for whatever reason, he never confronted the substance of her awesome, enigmatic thought in print. And the rest of his contemporaries were midgets or moderns. Meanwhile, as the Nietzschification of the world proceeded in overdrive — around us, and within us — Grant could hold to the eternal hope that had been given him. But he still had to bring the bad news: such hope could no longer be thought within the language of the modern *polis*, at least not by ordinary mortals. Hence the eternal was all but mute.

In the final essays written for *Technology and Empire*, Grant arrived at a terrible and original resolution of the matter. The task of philosophy now, *pace* Strauss, was not to think from outside modern nihilism. It was to articulate coherently the impossibility of doing so.

This he achieved.

*

What Grant managed was to conceptualize a fundamental problem in the present estate of thinking. This condition had come to obtain as the impersonal lay of the land after nihilism became self-conscious in Nietzsche, and after technological progress became problematic to itself throughout Western society. As a first approximation, the state of affairs can be characterized thus:

* Human beings are made to be claimed by the real.

* Yet so centrally have we become technique — in our doing, willing, and conceiving — that we can no longer think what it would mean, to be "claimed by the real." Our basic mental categories are now incommensurable with what those words point to; our minds no longer work that way.

* Yet we can't stop trying to think such a claim, because the world which our minds now are equipped to process is a world we can barely live in.

* We're thus in a permanent double bind, which produces characteristic short-circuits and deadends when we try to think about the whole. The eventual result is a rational muteness, a silence of reason.

I propose to call this state of affairs "Grant's Impasse." I mean by the term, not "a private muddle that George Grant got himself into," but rather "a civilisational quandary that George Grant charted." The impasse was already there, a necessary condition and limitation of contemporary thinking. Grant simply identified it. Hence the usage is parallel to terms like "Pike's Peak," "Halley's Comet," "Godel's Theorem."

Note also that "Grant's Impasse" is not a name for the overall nihilism which the liberal paradigm has carried within itself for centuries (based on the de-sacramentalisation of the world, and the relativity of all "values"). It names something more recent and limited: the set of mind-jamming contradictions which emerge when we try to think critically about technological civilisation now. Grant was not the first person to experience those contradictions. But as far as I'm aware, he was the first to make them problematic, to identify them as a necessary condition of modern thinking, which we probably cannot transcend. My reading in the field is far from systematic. But Grant's analysis of the estate of reason within the nihilism we inhabit is both more advanced and more fundamental than any other I've met.

Here's one way in which he characterized the central contradictions of the impasse :

> The difficulty then of those who seek substantive values by which to judge particular techniques is that they must generally think of such values within the massive assumptions of modern thought. Indeed even to think 'values' at all is to be within such assumptions. But the goal of modern moral striving — the building of free and equal human beings — leads inevitably back to a trust in the expansion of that very technology we are attempting to judge. The unfolding of modern society has not only required the criticism of all older standards of human excellence, but has also at its heart that trust in the overcoming of chance which leads us back to judge every human situation as being solvable in terms of technology. As moderns we have no standards by which to judge particular techniques, except standards welling up with our faith in technical expansion.[2]

Broadly put, then, the impasse is that any would-be critical thought about technology is bound to reproduce that technology in the methods and assumptions of our thinking. We can't abide the nihilism we're enmeshed in; yet we can't think our way out of it, because we can't stop recreating it in the very fabric of our thought.

*

A great deal of Grant's energy in the late 'sixties went into simply getting these things articulated. It must have required ferocious concentration. And, as one reader, I must say that twenty years on I'm still finding my way in the strange landscape he charted. As far as I can think his findings through, Grant uncovered two stages of the impasse — two "tightenings," I'd like to call them. His concern was to give true testimony, however, not just to create a taxonomy of mind-ruptures. So in distinguishing these "tightenings," I'll be supplying a more explicit shape to things than Grant himself presented.

The first tightening is one he grappled with in the passage I just cited. "As moderns we have no standards by which to judge particular techniques, except standards welling up with our faith in technical expansion." As always in Grant's writing on the impasse, this delineates a situation in which we find we can't think to the purpose we had intended. Our minds are checkmated.

In general terms, it takes this form. We want to analyze critically, or judge morally, some technique, or else some problem created by technology. (While Grant refers to "particular techniques," the only concrete examples in Technology and Empire, I believe, are found in "The University Curriculum," where he speaks of attempting to judge the newly technical disciplines of the knowledge industry.) To achieve such a critique, we turn to one of the ideas or standards that form part of the inherited repertoire for critical thought or moral judgment. But we then discover, on looking closer, that this outside arbiter or higher principle is no longer any such thing. In the course of the modern period, it has been transformed out of all recognition; it has become seamless with the technique we're trying to think about, in that both now arise from a common origin—broadly speaking, "technology" —and dissolve back into it. So it gives us no purchase whatsoever for critical thought. And when this happens enough times, the whole project of "thinking critically" or "judging morally" starts to founder. This is the first tightening of the impasse.

It could be likened to someone discovering they've become near-sighted, calling in an oculist to correct the defect, and finding that the oculist is near-sighted also, and to the same degree. To get a sense of how the mind eventually goes into gridlock, however, you'd have to imagine that we then call in a physiotherapist, an historian of visual perception, an eye surgeon, a psychologist, and discover that each suffers from the same near-sightedness as all the others.

Grant appears to have recognized this vicious circle while writing "The University Curriculum" in 1967. After that he returned to it often, explicating the ways in which it grows from our deepest technological fate. Here are two more formulations from *Technology and Empire*:

> The tight circle in which we live is this: our present forms of existence have sapped the ability to think about standards of excellence, and yet at the same time have imposed on us a standard in terms of which the human good is monolithically asserted. [3]

We live in the most realised technological society which has ever been....It might seem then that ... we might be the people best able to comprehend what it is to be so....Yet the very substance of our existing, which has made us the leaders in technique, stands as a barrier to any thinking which might be able to comprehend technique from beyond its own dynamic. [4]

*

These may appear to be extremely generalized, even abstract formulations. And it's true enough: they are. In the late 'sixties, Grant articulated the impasse by pressing through to the purest and most generic terms of its existing. Evidently this was how he was able to think its coherence at all.

That accomplished, some of his subsequent writing would be devoted to giving concrete examples of the first tightening, which he had described in such general terms here. After 1969, he would uncover in a succession of instances (such as "the liberal account of justice") the lineaments of the general impasse anatomized in "The University Curriculum," "In Defence of North America," and "A Platitude." This would not extend or recast the basic model, but it would bring it down to earth.

*

The second tightening of the impasse is explored primarily in the essay "A Platitude" (the final piece written for *Technology and Empire*). From the present perspective, these seven pages stand as the most advanced in all Grant's writing, his most unflinching gaze into the heart of darkness. He wrote them in witness, and he didn't go under. The question always was: what you could possibly write after ?

The strategy of thought which Grant depicts in this second tightening has changed. The thinker is no longer moving from "problem" to "critical/ethical solution" to "collapse of that solution" — finding that each new solution turns out to re-embody the problem. Instead he tries, in a scarcely imaginable gesture, to break directly out of the impasse, to think a more-than-liberal reality which he can identify as the thing he's deprived of — and discovers that he has skidded into white space, unthinkability, ground zero. He finds himself mute; if "reason" got brain-damaged in the first tightening, it is simply subtracted here, lobotomized. For at this advanced stage of the impasse, we find we can no longer name — not in the world of public discourse, predictably enough, but scarcely even to ourselves — the thing we lack, let alone trace its rational coherence. Here is how "A Platitude" explores this second tightening:

> We can hold in our minds the enormous benefits of technological society, but we cannot so easily hold the ways it may have deprived us, because technique is ourselves....
>
> It is difficult to think whether we are [now] deprived of anything essential to our happiness, just because the coming to be of the technological society has stripped us above all of the very systems of meaning which disclosed the highest purposes of man, and in terms of which, therefore, we could judge whether an absence of something was in fact a deprival.
>
> All coherent languages beyond those which serve the drive to unlimited freedom through technique have been broken up in the coming to be of what we are. Therefore it is impossible to articulate publicly any suggestion of loss, and perhaps even more frightening, almost impossible to articulate it to ourselves. We have been left with no words which cleave together and summon out of uncertainty the good of which we may sense the dispossession. The drive to the planetary technical future is in any case inevitable; but those who would try to divert, to limit, or even simply to stand in fear before some of its applications find themselves defenceless, because of the disappearance of any speech by which the continual changes involved in that drive could ever be thought of as deprivals.[6]

To listen for the intimations of deprival requires attempting a distinction between our individual history and any account which might be possible of what belongs to man as man.

Yet even as one says this, the words fade. The language of what belongs to man as man has long since been disintegrated. Have we not been told that to speak of what belongs to man as man is to forget that man creates himself in

history? How can we speak of excellences which define the
height for man, because what one epoch calls an excellence
another does not, and we can transcend such historical
perspectives only in the quantifiable?...We are back where
we began: all languages of good except the language of the
drive to freedom have disintegrated, so it is just to pass some
antique wind to speak of goods that belong to man as
man....[7]

*

In this second tightening, then, the mind is not trying to analyse or
judge a "particular technique." Instead, it forages for categories
simply to *name* the unconditionally claiming realities which modern
thought has ruled inadmissible, and to which we have consequently
lost rational access. And this engenders an all-but-withering despair,
for we cannot find any such categories unchanged by modernity. We
are necessarily mute as rational beings, even in the privacy of our best
intuitions.

Yet Grant's writing does not come to rest in hopelessness. What
he opens himself to, in "A Platitude," is a mode of silence which might
mediate (in his beautiful phrase) "intimations of deprival." Let us
return to the end of the previous quotation:

We are back where we began: all languages of good except
the language of the drive to freedom have disintegrated, so
it is just to pass some antique wind to speak of goods that
belong to man as man. Yet the answer is also the same: if we
cannot so speak, then we can either only celebrate [the
technological imperative] or stand in silence before that
drive. Only in listening for the intimations of deprival can
we live critically in the dynamo. [8]

The second option, to "stand in silence before that drive," is
presented somewhat cryptically. In point of fact, to "stand in silence"
is not just a single option. Grant is very clear that we have been brought
to silence; the checkmate of other-than-liberal rational language is
complete. Yet the silence itself can be of two kinds. It can be a muteness
of acquiescence, of turning one's face to the wall—the sort of defeatism
with which he himself was sometimes taxed, by people incapable of
reading more than how-to manuals and bank statements. The alter-

nate form of silence is one in which we "listen for intimations of deprival." It is this latter silence from which he speaks in "A Platitude," and which he recommends in fear and trembling.

But what are these "intimations of deprival?" It is in keeping with Grant's penchant for pure generic analysis, during the several years in which he diagnosed the impasse definitively, that "A Platitude" doesn't contain a single example. There are passages elsewhere in *Technology and Empire*, however, which suggest what he has in mind. My favourite is the moving summary of his encounter with an older contemplative tradition in Europe (presumably at Oxford and during World War Two). There, he says, he "felt the remnants of a Christianity which was more than simply the legitimising of progress and which still held in itself the fruits of contemplation." By this he means, not so much the vestigially authentic theology he was then studying, as:

> things more deeply in the stuff of everyday living which remain long after they can no longer be thought: public and private virtues having their point beyond what can in any sense be called socially useful; commitments to love and friendship which lie rooted in a realm outside the calculable; of a partaking in the beautiful not seen as the product of human creativity; amusements and ecstasies not seen as the enemies of reason. [9]

*

Now let me read you a piece which wrestles with the intimations of deprival in its own way, that of poetic meditation. It's called "The Gods."

THE GODS

I

Who, now, can speak of gods —
their strokes and carnal voltage,
old ripples of presence a space ago
archaic eddies of being?

Perhaps a saint could speak their names.
Or maybe some
noble claustrophobic spirit,
crazed by the flash and
vacuum of modernity,
could reach back, ripe for
gods and a hot lobotomy.
But being none of these, I sit
bemused by the sound of the words.
For a man no longer moves
through coiled ejaculations of
meaning;
we dwell within
taxonomies, equations, paradigms
which deaden the world and now in our
heads, though less in our inconsistent lives,
the tickle of cosmos is gone.
Though what would a god be *like* —
would he shop at Dominion?
Would he know about DNA molecules? and keep little gold
stars, for when they behaved?
. . . It is not from simple derision
that the imagination snickers. But faced with an alien
reality it
stammer, it races & churns
for want of a common syntax and
lacking a possible language
who, now, can speak of gods? for random example
a bear to our ancestors, and even to
grope in a pristine hunch back to that way of being on earth
is nearly beyond me.

II

And yet —
in the middle of one more day, in a clearing maybe   sheer
godforce,
calm on the lope of its pads
furred   hot-breathing   erect, at ease, catastrophic
harsh waves of stink, the
dense air clogged with its roaring and
ripples of power fork through us:

31

hair gone electric   quick
          pricklish glissando, the
skin   mind skidding, balking is
         HAIL
and it rears foursquare and we are jerked and owned and
         forgive us   and
    brought to a welter, old
force & destroyer and
         do not destroy us!
    or if it seems good,
       destroy us.

Thus, the god against us in clear air.
       And there are gentle gods —
       as plain as
   light that
        rises from lake-face,
     melding with light
that skips like a stepping-stone spatter
       down to
        evoke it,
till blue embraces blue, and lake and sky
       are miles of indigenous climax —
such grace in the shining air.

All gods, all gods and none of them
       domesticated angels, chic of spat & wing
on ten-day tours of earth. And if
to speak of 'gods' recalls those antique
      wind-up toys, forget the gods as well:
       tremendum rather,
dimension of otherness, come clear
     in each familiar thing — in
outcrop, harvest, hammer, beast and
      caught in that web of otherness
   we too endure & we
    worship.
Men lived among that force, a space ago.

Or,
whirling it reins into phase through us, good god it can
     use us, power in tangible
    dollops invading the roots of the
    hair, the gap behind the neck,
power to snag, coax bully exalt into presence
     clean gestures of meaning among the traffic of earth,
and until it lobs us aside, pale snot poor
       rags we
    also can channel the godforce.
                  Yet still not

  abject: not
     heaven & wistful hankering — I mean
    the living power, inside
        and, that sudden that
     plumb!
    Men lived in such a space.

III

    I do say gods.
  But that was time ago, technology
      happened and what has been withdrawn
  I do not understand, the absent ones,
though many then too were bright & malevolent and
     crushed things that mattered,
and where they have since been loitering I scarcely comprehend,
    and least of all can I fathom, you powers I
  seek and no doubt cheaply arouse and
     who are you?
    how I am to salute you, nor how contend with your being
for I do not aim to make prize-hungry words (and stay back!) I want
    the world to be real and
     it will not,
for to secular men there is not given the glory of tongues, yet it is
    better to speak in silence than squeak in the gab of the age
    and if I cannot tell your terrifying
  praise, now Hallmark gabble and chintz nor least of all
    what time and dimensions your naked incursions
    announced, you scurrilous powers yet
    still I stand against this bitch of a shrunken time

                    in semi-faithfulness
and whether you are godhead or zilch or daily ones like before
            your strike our measure still and still you
                endure as my murderous fate,
                                            though I
        do not know you.

III

In Grant's writing in the late sixties, the intimations of deprival are fitful at best. The first reality for the philosophic mind is the muteness of reason in a structurally nihilist civilisation. And its first necessity is to bear witness to that silence.

In *Technology and Empire*, Grant anatomized two stages or tightenings in the impasse of reason. The first was the checkmate we encounter when we try to analyze or judge a specific technique, and find that every standard we invoke is itself an expression of technological thinking. The second was the checkmate we encounter when we try to represent directly to ourselves the more-than-liberal reality whose loss we sense, and find that our minds lack any categories to articulate such a thing.

This analysis of rational deadlock in the West could well come to be recognized as indispensable, strategic, the substantial step which had to be taken at this juncture. But there was a price to pay for such lucid news of extremis: Grant's Impasse came to be consciously home. As its explorer virtually keened (in a sentence added in 1969 to the end of "Canadian Fate and Imperialism"):

> What is worth doing in the midst of this barren twilight is the incredibly difficult question. [10]

Mind you, the problem is not just one of being demoralized by the impasse, of suffering a private paralysis of the will. That is certainly a danger. But the real dilemma lies deeper, and might be framed as follows:

* How many times can philosophic thought articulate the rationale of its own closure? Yet,

* If the impasse is real, what other project of thought is there to pursue?

That was the dilemma Grant would face, unremittingly, after his groundbreaking investigations of 1967-69.

*

This completes our examination of Grant's Impasse, as it was presented in the extraordinary meditations written in the late sixties. Let me identify several lines of enquiry which open up next, without trying to pursue them in any way.

Two are concerned with situating the analysis of the impasse within Grant's entire body of work.

* Grant published three more books in the nineteen years that remained to him. How do their projects of thought relate to his exploration of the impasse?

* We know from statements in interviews that Grant had become a Christian in 1942, and remained one throughout his life. What did his religious faith consist of? And how did his Christianity (or for that matter, his Platonism) relate to his exploration of the silencing of reason?

Two others are my own response to the difficult terrain Grant opened up.

* Can we say anything coherent about the experience of ineffability — that is, of encountering the world moment to moment as valuative, while lacking any rational language in which to articulate such experience?

* Is it possible that the experience of rational deadend can become a contemplative discipline, have affinities with the "negative way" of one branch of Western spirituality? (This is the branch represented by such figures as Meister Eckhart, the anonymous author of The Cloud of Unknowing, and St. John of the Cross.)

These are questions I hope to return to. For now, let me end
with three poems of ending and beginning; of leaving and coming
home. They're from a work in progress called "Nightwatch."

THREE POEMS FROM "NIGHTWATCH"

Hush hush, little
      wanderer. Hush your
    weary load.   Who touched down
once, once, once in America —
and over you flashed the net!
And they said, You will forget your name and
      your home and
it was so: already I had forgotten.

But how did I come to be here?
    This place is not my place;
these ways are not my ways.   I
    do not understand their
consumer index; their value-free techniques; their GNP —
      weird abstract superstitions, and
when I settled in to stay,
    it felt unclean.

Son of the house!
For they fed me and
      dressed me in silks, they
trussed me with first-world pay.
They poured sweet liqueurs on my tongue and said,
   Sing the old ways,
      sing of your roots....
What have I sunk to?

Though they hem me with filigree,
         this is not my country.
Though I bask on a diamond leash it is not my home.
But what am I doing here still, how long will I
         desecrate the name?
   Who was born to
         another estate, in a
   place I have nearly forgotten.

How late, my
       life, will I
         dream in the malls of America? —
crippled by plenty.   How
       long will I put off the time?

For years I thought I was
         gold, gold in a
 secret place — and
         one day, incognito,
the prince my soul would come and steal me away.

Fairy tales! a blanket of
       fairy tales!
But there are great, uncaring
spaces, and the winds whip through from there and they
       scour what is.

    (Gingerly,
         soberly,
    home. In
  a torrent of
       riddance....)

And so I woke up,
and I knew, It is time to get shy of America.
    Time to come out of here,
for we do not need these burnt-out dreams infesting our lives;
   we must quit them, before we die.

When first we came to this land,
there was a promise: a
beacon: a city on a hill, white clapboard new
zion perpetual lookout;
and in the streets, a rhythm and deals.
Lashings of brave blue sky,
larrup of freedom, of Gunplay & God —
High on a noose of glory, and
laced with encomium.
It took us in.
Cheap beer. New paradigms.   And we came
tearing down the street
when we heard that dirty beat,
crying, *America, land of pure real estate!*
imperial vista! republic of raw material!
America turn us to gold....

•
Now: grain rots in the inland harbours. And
far in the boondocks, our masters prescribe a regime
of torture & famine,
famine & torture,
while here in the heartland of empire, the immaterial senses
atrophy, grown over.... Through
generations of captivity, we have
cherished our miniscule percs; and
in the ache of our
exile we
scoffed at the rumours of home,
crediting only   USA/America   USSR/America   Babylon planet,
though in the end we stammered, "Earth, green earth and
dying — in our
lifetime, likely,
goodbye."

Mostly we have to keep low.
But also it's good to come to be hunger pangs,
taking the
shape sheer craving makes.   And it will go

hard with those who have found their ease in America.
I will come out!
For there is a calling, namable by
silence; and a
track, a path of no-
going. There is an
exodus, though mainly
one by one by one.
I will come out!
Whose price is my life.
And though my tongue is blind, and I balk and have no maps *I*
will come out.

NOTES

1   George Grant, "In Defence of North America," *Technology and Empire: Perspectives on North America.* (Toronto: Anansi, 1969), p. 40.

2   Ibid., p. 34.

3   Grant, "The University Curriculum," op.cit.*supra*, p. 131.

4   Grant, "In Defence of North America," op.cit.*supra*, p. 40.

5   Grant, "A Platitude", op.cit.*supra*, p. 137.

6   Ibid., p. 139.

7   Ibid., p. 140-141.

8   Ibid., p. 141.

9   Grant, "In Defence of North America," op.cit.*supra*, p. 36.

10   Grant, "Canadian Fate and Imperialism," op.cit.*supra*, p. 78.

PART II

THE POLITICAL INDEPENDENCE OF CANADA

ONE LAST CHANCE:
THE LEGACY OF LAMENT FOR A NATION

Mel Hurtig

What I propose to do in this paper is to look briefly at what George Grant had to say in *Lament for a Nation*, try to summarize his conclusions, with particular reference to the Canadian establishment and the Liberal and Conservative parties, and then look at where we are in Canada today, in the final months of the 1980s, at the start of the last decade of the century that was supposed to have belonged to Canada.

To begin with, I'd like to repeat what I said last February in a talk in Calgary, entitled "The Last Chance for Canada" (a topic I shall come back to at the end of my paper):

> George Grant's small paperback book deeply influenced a generation of Canadians, including many of our most respected public figures and leading politicians in all three of our major political parties. When *Lament for a Nation* was first published by McClelland and Stewart in 1965, it had a tiny first printing and virtually no advertising. In the space of a few months it was reprinted several times and new editions appeared in 1970 and in 1978, and now again in 1989. *Lament for a Nation* was subtitled *The Defeat of Canadian Nationalism*.

> George Grant eloquently, passionately and sadly, proclaimed that Canada had ceased to be a nation, and that U.S. dominance clearly precluded the ability of Canadians to build the more ordered, independent and special society they had so long ago aspired to.

43

Ironically, George Grant's *Lament*, along with the exuberance of Canada's centennial two years later, became the spark for a new and intense period of Canadian self-confidence and Canadian nationalism. The 'new nationalism' was lively, controversial, and relatively brief, extending from the late 1960s to perhaps 1982.

It is interesting to look back, a generation later, at the reviews *Lament for a Nation* received upon publication. About a third were complimentary, most were mixed, and more than a few were downright hostile. "Exaggerated, one hopes..." was a common theme. "Too pessimistic by far!" was another. Grant was roundly criticized for writing in terms of inevitability, in terms of an inexorable process - "inexorable" was one of his favourite words. I shall return to this word later.

Mordecai Richler, the professional anti-Canadian, reviewed the book in *Bookweek* in October of 1965:

> Canada, Grant concludes, is a satellite. Yes, of course, but its independence, it seems to me, was always illusory .... to be a Canadian ... I think, was to turn pinched backs on the most exciting events on the continent, and to be a party to one of the most foolish, unnecessary and artificial of frontiers.

Of course most Canadians thought otherwise. Lister Sinclair summed it up nicely on a CBC broadcast in 1965: [*Lament for a Nation*] is a work of prophetic power and insight which changed a whole generation's view of Canada." Unfortunately, as we now know, it *wasn't* exactly a whole generation. But it was an important part of it. Gad Horowitz, I think, put it well when he suggested that there was something really unique about a conservative philosopher who was at the same time radical in a way that makes leftists fond of him.

George Grant was very influential in my life and his work bears rereading. I came away from *Lament* with some of the same misgivings I had twenty-four years ago. Mostly, though, when I closed the pages on this little book, I felt a great sense of irony: how right he was. And in some ways how wrong he was. But, what a great Canadian he was!

Make no mistake, *Lament for a Nation* was no mere warning, as some have suggested, no sounding of the alarm. Grant spelled it out clearly: "To lament is to cry out at the death or at the dying of something loved. This lament mourns the end of Canada as a sovereign state."[1] Later, he reiterates: "... Canada cannot survive as a sovereign nation.... our nation was not a viable entity."[2] Again, "The 1957 election was the Canadian people's last gasp of nationalism."[3] Now, "We find ourselves like fish left on the shores of a drying lake. The element necessary to our existence has passed away."[4] And, perhaps the most important paragraph in the book:

> Only nationalism could provide the political incentive for planning; only planning could restrain the victory of continentalism.... no such combination was possible and therefore our nation was bound to disappear.[5]

For George Grant, decisions made by Liberal governments, beginning in the 1940s, made it impossible to have an independent nation, our own defence or foreign policy, or even a distinct culture. Towards the end of the book comes the quote that so many of us used in speeches during the last half of the 1960s, and for the next two decades. There is no uncertainty in these words:

> Canada has ceased to be a nation, but its formal political existence will not end quickly. Our social and economic blending into the American empire will continue apace, but political union will probably be delayed.[6]

So, who was to blame?

Clearly it was the establishment and the Liberal party. There was little doubt. There was also little doubt they were one and the same. Over and over again the elite, the establishment, money, power, the ruling classes, the wealthy, the capitalists and the corporations are singled out: "... the Canadian ruling class looks across the border for its final authority in both politics and culture."[7] The country's "economic self-seekers had never been the ones to care about Canada as a nation."[8] Again,

> most of them [the economically powerful] made more money by being the representatives of American capi-

talism and setting up branch plants. No class in Canada more welcomed the American managers than the established wealthy of Montreal and Toronto.... They lost nothing essential to the principle of their lives in losing their country.[9]

Otherwise put, "in its simplest form, continentalism is the view of those who do not see what all the fuss is about."[10] E. P. Taylor is quoted as saying: "Canadian nationalism! How old fashioned can you get!"[11]

Historian Kenneth McNaught, reviewing Grant's book along with John Porter's *The Vertical Mosaic*, summed them up this way: "... American corporate capitalism was permitted free access to our resources and investment areas so that a majority of the Canadian power elite now identifies its interests with those of American corporations."[12] And of course, McNaught wrote, "The wealthy assumed it was natural there should be an identity of interests between themselves and the Liberals." In fact, "the Liberal Party is the political instrument for the Canadian establishment."

Grant wrote that "the villains of my book" were liberalism, Liberals and Lester Pearson.[13] "The politicians, the businessmen and the civil servants worked harmoniously together" to achieve the Liberal policy of "integration as fast as possible and at all costs. No other consideration was allowed to stand in the way."[14] As Grant asserted, "The Liberals openly announced that our resources were at the disposal of continental capitalism.... they identified their branch-plant society with the Kingdom of Heaven" and their policy was "satellite status to the United States."[15] And finally: "...for twenty years... the Liberal party had been pursuing policies that led inexorably to the disappearance of Canada."[16]

As someone who, sixteen years ago, left the Liberal party because of its continentalism, I find it difficult to quarrel with this part of Grant's analysis. The policies of MacKenzie King and C.D. Howe led Canada firmly into the American embrace. The brief "economic nationalism" of Pierre Trudeau (if indeed that is what it was) all but disappeared during the last years of his final term in office. The policies necessary for reclaiming the Canadian economy were abandoned. In its last years the Foreign Investment Review Agency became a joke, a rubber stamp.

* * *

So far, I think, it's easy to agree with most of what Grant wrote. However, when we come to the Conservative party, the conservative traditions he admired, the British connection and British traditions, many of us must now regard his faith as misplaced. Obviously, it is not the traditions that betrayed George Grant, but rather the continentalist Canadian neo-conservatives who were swept into power in 1984. Think of Brian Mulroney, John Crosbie, Pat Carney, Joe Clark and Michael Wilson when Grant writes that Canadian conservatives never stood on an abstract appeal to free enterprise but that they were willing to use the government to protect the common good. Or, that he greatly resented the identification of the word "conservative" with the right of individuals to make money any way they want[17]. And, as he makes clear: "... the existence of Canada depended on a clear definition of conservatism."[18]

Think of the Conservative party of Brian Mulroney in terms of Kenneth McNaught's review of Lament for a Nation in *Saturday Night*, August 1965:

> It is now beyond doubt that Conservatives, in recognizing the desperate need of a counterbalance to the American continental pull, have always been the more nationalist of the two major parties... . Genuine Conservatives... were prepared to use government not just to guarantee free competition... but to limit private intrusions upon the public interest. They established a tradition of public enterprise in transportation, communication and power development.[19]

David Cayley, in his excellent Canadian Broadcasting Corporation series on George Grant, "The Moving Image of Eternity" (January 27, 1986), put it this way: "Grant recognized that in Canada, Conservatives have often had to behave like Socialists in the interest of national survival." Instead, a new generation of Conservatives, raised in the boardrooms of the multinationals' branch plants, or in the head offices of Canadian conglomerates, have abandoned a century of Conservative traditions for their own variations of Reaganomics and Thatcherism, and grabbed the mantle of continentalism with glee.

Think of Peter Lougheed, Don Getty, Grant Devine. Think of Bill Davis and Brian Peckford. Think of the Business Council on National Issues and the *Globe and Mail*, or *The Financial Post*. The Conservatives of today, the Conservatives since John Diefenbaker, hardly resemble the conservatism George Grant admired. On the contrary, *at best*, in terms of nationalism and continentalism, there is little to distinguish the record of Canadian conservatism during the past quarter century from the liberalism George Grant so despised. At the worst, we have the blatant sell-out of a country, beginning in 1984. Perhaps the Liberals built the coffin. The Conservatives of Brian Mulroney closed the lid and nailed it shut.

* * *

I see little reason to dwell on Grant's enthusiasm for British conservatism and British traditions today. Recent history has made much of what he had to say relatively meaningless more than two decades later. Some of us felt uncomfortable with the British connection, as he described it, back in 1965, especially in relation to French Canada, and certainly also in relation to western Canada. But the transformation of England under Margaret Thatcher, and the resulting abandonment of so many of the true conservative characteristics and traditions Grant admired, now make this section of the book as ironic as the previously described faith in Canadian Conservatives. In fairness to Grant, he himself recognized the changes taking place in Britain.

In relation to French Canada, though, Grant was prophetic:

"They will ... build a society in which the right of the common good restrains the freedom of the individual."[20] As he clearly recognized, "Some of the extreme actions of French Canadians in their efforts to preserve their society will drive other Canadians to identify themselves more closely with their southern neighbours than with the strange and alien people of Quebec."[21]

For those of us who fought so long and so hard to defeat the Free Trade Agreement (which should really be called the Americanization-of-Canada Agreement, the ACA), this last quote is a bitter paradox. On the one hand, Bill 178 and the Meech Lake Accord are producing a strong anti-Quebec feeling across much of Canada. On the other hand, Quebec's blind faith in Brian Mulroney and Robert Bourassa in the 1988 federal election defeated our efforts. Today, incredibly, support for joining the United States is higher in Quebec than in any other part of Canada. This is not to blame Quebec for what has happened to the Canadian dream. The real blame is to be directed at the federal politicians who failed to understand that selling off the country and abandoning our own culture was hardly likely to inspire Quebecois to identify with the rest of Canada.

For Grant, even "French-Canadian nationalism is a last-ditch stand. The French on this continent will at least disappear from history with more than the smirks and whimpers of their English-speaking compatriots - with their flags flying and, indeed, with some guns blazing."[22]

My main point is this: I think that George Grant was likely wrong when he said, back in 1965, that the dream of Canada had ended, that it was too late, that the forces of continentalism were by then inexorable and irreversible. We now know that the 1957 election was hardly "the Canadian people's last gasp of nationalism."[23]

But that is not my main conclusion. My main conclusion is that if there was any doubt about the validity of George Grant's central theme in 1965, there can be very little doubt today. Today, late in 1989, Canada's situation is infinitely worse than it was a quarter of a century ago. Today, the forces of continentalism, both within and outside Canada, are far more powerful, more confident and more in charge than ever before in our history. Big business in Canada, now more than ever before, is firmly in control. To its proponents, the survival of Canada is of little or no concern. Their unprecedented and most successful intervention in the 1988 election has whetted their appetite for more. The recent Revenue Canada rulings will make spending by big business in 1988 look like petty cash, compared to what they will pour into the 1992-93 campaign.

And big business, now more than ever before, owns and controls most of our country. A small handful of Canadian and foreign corporations make most of the sales and most of the profits and own most of the corporate assets across the nation. This concentration of ownership has increased dramatically in recent years, and will continue to increase in the future. These same corporations are the ones that backed the so-called Free Trade Agreement. They are also the very same corporations which put up most of the money for Brian Mulroney's 1984 and 1988 election campaigns, and which will put up most of the money for the 1990 Liberal leadership campaign, and for the 1992-93 federal election campaign.

The print media in Canada, with few exceptions, are now clearly continentalist and Conservative. The two daily national newspapers, from which much of the local press and electronic media spin many of their stories and editorials, are both far to the right and lacking in objectivity. With two exceptions, the newspapers of the Southam Press support the continentalism of the Mulroney government, and the Thompson and Sun papers make E.P. Taylor look like a nationalist by comparison. Maclean-Hunter, if you can imagine, despite their posturing to the contrary, and pretence at objectivity, supports continentalism. To read *Maclean's* and Conrad Black's *Saturday Night* is to weep.

At the same time, the pervasive influence of network and cabled American television is probably the most underestimated development in modern Canadian history. Travel across Canada and turn on the television sets in Inuvik and Saskatoon, St John's, and dozens of other communities across the nation, to satellite TV, direct from Detroit, and you will better understand how misplaced George Grant's faith was when he wrote, optimistically:

"Most helpful is that among the young... the desire for independence is greater than for many generations."[24] Not only is this statement now obviously and pathetically untrue, but many of our young have little or no idea that Canada's independence is even an issue, let alone seriously threatened. The virtual absence of university, college, and high school students from the great "free trade" debate, and from the crucial election of 1988, is perhaps the surest sign that while George Grant's faith in the young was in error, his prophecy about Canada was not.

Today, Canada has a degree of foreign ownership that would not be tolerated in any other developed nation in the world. While it is not yet back to the appalling levels of the late sixties and early seventies, it is now not only rapidly headed in that direction, but certain to reach new record levels before the next election. (Canada's foreign indebtedness compared to Gross Domestic Product, was only 18 percent when *Lament for a Nation* was published in 1965. Today it is 39 percent!). But now, the Americanization-of-Canada Agreement makes it impossible for Canadians to reverse the process, without abrogating the entire agreement. American corporations will continue to gobble up hundreds of Canadian companies each and every year, regardless of how Canadians may feel about the takeover of their country. The manufacturing industry, the petroleum industry, the chemical industry, the automotive industry and dozens of other crucial industries are already heavily dominated by American multinational corporations. By 1992 or 1993 many other Canadian industries will be firmly controlled from abroad. And the captains of these industries, the Canadian compradors and their foreign employers, will continue to dominate the "Canadian" Petroleum Association, the "Canadian" Manufacturers' Association, the Business Council on National Issues, the Conference Board of Canada and the Canadian-American Committee.

They will continue to fund the continentalist, biased C.D. Howe Institute, the Fraser Institute and the Canada West Foundation, whose slanted, pre-ordained publications are accepted as unquestioned gospel by all but a handful of Canadian journalists. Sadly, people like Marjorie Nichols, David Crane and Don McGillivray represent a tiny minority. The dismal failure of the vast majority of Canadian journalists to understand the pervasive, nation-shackling ramifications of the Free Trade Agreement, is a sad commentary on the state of Canadian journalism.

There is not enough space here to discuss the dubious role of Canadian banks and other financial institutions in this process, nor the role of the provinces, the deterioration of the Department of External Affairs, the growing influence of multinational corporations in Canadian politics, the gradual and destructive undermining of the CBC, and the debilitating provisions concerning monopolies, subsidies, energy, resource- sharing and other items covered in the Americanization-of-Canada Agreement. Collectively they act as an iron straitjacket on the democratic process in Canada, at all three levels of elected government. George Grant wrote accurately that "The power of Ottawa has to be skilfully used by politicians to balance the enormous anti-national forces concentrated in the economic capitals of Toronto and Montreal."[25] Not only do today's Conservative politicians have no desire to use such power, but, thanks to the ACA, they no longer could use it, even if they wished to. (And the "anti-national forces" are now located in all areas of Canada, not just in Toronto and Montreal.)

If you think about Meech Lake, think, too, about this from *Lament for a Nation*:

> The espousing by... Canadian 'conservatives' of greater authority for [the provinces] has always had a phoney ring about it, unless it is coupled with an appeal for the break-up of continental corporations. Decentralized government and continental corporations can lead in only one direction.[26]

Since *Lament for a Nation* was published much has changed. In terms of the survival of Canada, much has worsened. George Grant used to say that to live with courage in the world is always better than retreat or disillusion. Thus, "to live with courage is a virtue, whatever one may think of the dominant assumptions of one's age."[27] And he was fond of quoting theologian Richard Hooker: "'Posterity may know we have not loosely through silence, permitted things to pass away as in a dream.'"[28]

Or have we? I have said before that I believe there is, perhaps, one last chance for Canada, the election of 1992-1993. In my opinion, this will indeed be our very last chance. The next three years of the accelerated integration process will in itself be very difficult to reverse, perhaps impossible. But, if the Mulroney government wins the next election, it will certainly be forever too late to alter the course of the nation. Canada will have become so dependent, so vulnerable, so harmonized, so owned and controlled by foreign corporations that if in 1992-1993 the Conservatives are re-elected, the dream of Canada will surely be over once and for all.

And should there be a Liberal minority government? I have some reservations. The Liberal party of today is not made up solely of people like Lloyd Axworthy, Herb Gray and Sheila Copps, who could be counted on to stand up to those who would sell our country out to the highest foreign bidders. On the contrary, there are signs that the old continentalist domination of the Liberal party could return after the next election, if the Liberals found themselves in a majority position.

Could the New Democratic Party form the next government? Only the most optimistic social democrat would forecast such an event today. I have recently spent a great deal of time with many of the leadership hopefuls in both the Liberal and NDP parties. Some are good personal friends. Some I admire greatly. However, looking at the likely outcome of the two leadership conventions, and looking ahead to the results of the next federal election, today I can see only one scenario that would allow our country to survive. And it will likely be a very difficult scenario to achieve.

As early as 1985, thousands of Canadians across our country began the battle against the Mulroney government's intention to sign a comprehensive free trade agreement with the United States. We formed new organizations and impressive, unprecedented alliances. With totally inadequate funding, we fought for the hearts and minds of Canadians, in by far the most important battle of our lives. In every respect but one, we won that battle. In 1985 and early 1986 70 percent to 80 percent of Canadians supported "free trade," whatever that was supposed to mean. By November of 1988, just before the election, the largest public opinion poll taken on the subject, showed that 51 percent of Canadians were opposed to the Mulroney deal, and only 39 percent were in favour. We won the battles, but we lost the war. Winning the hearts and minds of Canadians is meaningless, if you lose the most important poll of all, the federal election. In constituency after constituency the Progressive Conservative (PC) candidate came up the middle to win the riding. Look, for example, at Regina-Wascana:

PC	15,339
NDP	14,829
	}29,633
Lib	14,804

or Vancouver Centre:

PC	23,620
NDP	23,351
Lib	14,467

or Rosedale in Toronto:

PC	22,704
NDP	22,624
Lib	8,266

A *single day's work* in these three ridings, in a campaign of strategic voting, would have defeated three Conservative candidates. But it is hardly that simple in a nation-wide federal election. Hindsight is always easy. For there to be a strategic "Vote for Canada" campaign in the federal election of 1992-93 there would have to be: a) an organization such as the Council of Canadians taking the leadership, or a new national organization formed to plan the campaign - perhaps a League of Canadian Voters, or some such; b) a very substantial sum of money raised to finance sophisticated advance polling, and to communicate with the electorate; c) concentration on no more than forty key ridings where appropriate Liberal or NDP candidates could be elected; d) conscription of all the forces - the teachers, nurses, churches, nationalists, senior citizens, and so on - that joined together in the Pro-Canada Movement, an organization representing over ten million Canadians.

Support for the Liberal and NDP candidates must be carefully balanced, especially if the new Liberal leader is by then perceived to have continentalist inclinations. (Last fall, in Cambridge Ontario, the local Liberal candidate in the last federal election asked Jean Chretien what he would do about the Free Trade Agreement. Mr. Chretien's reply was brief and to the point: "You can't break up an omelette that's been set.")

The objective would be a minority government. Such a campaign would be expensive, difficult, and quite impossible to guarantee. But in my opinion, there is *no other alternative* for the survival of Canada. There are dozens of reasons why it could fail. But again, I personally know of no other choice.

If a minority government is elected in the next federal election, I hope it would have as its four main priorities: (1) a careful examination of proportional election laws in nations around the world, and the adoption of a proportional election system that would much more fairly represent the true wishes of the Canadian electorate; (2) the introduction of a bill into the House of Commons that would immediately halt the foreign takeover of Canadian companies until such time as the new government is prepared to evolve and implement new policies in this area; (3) a change in Canada's election expenses laws putting limits on spending, during federal elections, by those outside the direct political process. Such limits would apply to all of us, and are essential if the democratic process is to function as intended. Why have limits on parties, candidates and constituencies when big business can go out and buy elections? (4) the elimination of Americanization-of-Canada Agreement. The Mulroney government bargained away our country. We will have to reclaim it.

George Grant said "A society only articulates itself as a nation through some common intention among its people."[29] The largest question of all is this: can we still find such a common intention in Canada? I believe we can. I believe that deep in the hearts of Canadians there is a pride, a thankfulness, and a strong desire to continue as a nation. There are dozens of important reasons why we should do so. But .... Grant said of *Lament* that "This book was written too much from anger and too little from irony."[30] Looking back today, I say there is now too much irony, and too little anger.

In other countries students and workers, academics, small business persons and mothers would be marching in the streets, flags flying. Just before he died George Grant paraphrased himself in an interview on the CBC: "It is surely a nobler stance to go down with all flags flying and all guns blazing than to be quietly led... into the American mass." This, from a Canadian, conservative, religious philosopher!

Earlier, I mentioned Grant's use of the word "inexorable." Shortly after the crushing election of November 1988, a rather remarkable thing happened. I was placing a number of phone calls to prepare for a paper I was writing. One day I talked to a former minister of External Affairs, a former head of the Science Council of Canada, and a Toronto political scientist who is widely known for his writings on Canadian-American relations. My question was this: *Is it now too late?* Each of them said, sadly, that it *was* too late. The process was now "inexorable." I personally do not believe that to be true. But it is very, very close to being true. Canada has *one last chance*, the next federal election. Politics of the status quo will not do. If the country we love is to survive there must be new approaches to *direct* involvement in the political process. Nothing else will do.

Such new approaches will have to reflect our place internationally. I am a great internationalist, I've always been a strong supporter of the United Nations, the Hague, and the General Agreement on Tariffs and Trade. Canada was one of the pioneer forces in the GATT and I think we have prospered enormously under it. It is infinitely better for us to resolve trade disputes under international law than under American law, as will be the case under the new panels established by the Free Trade Agreement. Moreover, we have not done too badly under the GATT. We have lost a couple of disputes, but at least with the GATT we are dealing with countries that have similar concerns to our own in international trade matters. In a bilateral situation, however, with a stronger, economically more powerful United States; where on every second trade tribunal an American is going to be the fifth person constituting a majority; where the vast majority of complaints coming before us will be American complaints; and where the vast majority of decisions relating to the bilateral agreement will emerge from American complaints: we are ultimately going to be the losers. This will become evident when decisions are made in the fish processing and steel rail cases.

But that's not the most important point I want to make. If we are a satellite of another country, we cannot play the role in the world community that most of us aspire to. We cannot have a foreign policy that evolves from our own people and a defence policy that evolves from our own people. We cannot work to strengthen international institutions such as the GATT, fight for a stronger United Nations, and play a more independent role in many of the things that we will face in international relations. We are heading for a situation in which it will be impossible for us to have independent foreign and defence policies, or independent economic policies where we determine our own interest rate policies, or monitor policies relating to our social programs. We cannot play these kinds of roles if we are simply a branch-plant economy and a satellite of another country. And once again, we're firmly headed in that direction.

In conclusion, there can be no question that George Grant was a prophet. But so far his followers have failed — not because they are in the minority, but because they have used the wrong tactics. It remains to be seen whether or not they can learn from the bitter lessons of 1988. They have one last chance.

NOTES

1   George Grant, *Lament for a Nation — The Defeat of Canadian Nationalism.* (Ottawa: Carleton University Press, 1989), p. 2.

2   Ibid., p. 86.

3   Ibid., p. 5.

4   Ibid., p. 4.

5   Ibid., p. 15.

6   Ibid., p. 86.

7   Ibid., p. 9.

8   Ibid., p. 34.

9   Ibid., p. 47.

10   Ibid., p. 90.

11   Ibid., p. 42.

12   Kenneth McNaught, "Review of Lament for a Nation," *Saturday Night,* August 1965.

13   Grant, *Lament for a Nation,* p. viii.

14   Ibid., p. 41.

15   Ibid., p. 11.

16   Ibid., p. 4.

17   Ibid., p. 65, 70.

18   Ibid., p. 24.

19   McNaught, op. cit. supra, p.

20   Grant, op. cit. *supra*, p. 76.

21   Ibid., p. 91.

22   Ibid., p. 76.

23   Ibid., p. 5.

24   Ibid., p. viii.

25   Ibid., p. 18.

26   Ibid., p. 77.

27   Ibid., p. 96-97.

28   Ibid., p. 6.

29   Ibid., p. 68.

30   Ibid., p. x.

ON GEORGE GRANT'S NATIONALISM

David Warren

A man can live three days without food,
but without poetry, never!

Baudelaire

I

I should make clear my qualifications and disqualifications for speaking about George Grant. I have no academic credentials, and no rigorous training in philosophical method or vocabulary, and thus all the usual failings of an autodidact, plus a few that are peculiar to my own hot-headed temperament. But I have immense respect for the discipline of philosophy, which I take to consist of the reckless pursuit of truth beyond every partial truth and semblance. I have read Grant carefully, not with perfect understanding, but often in nearly perfect sympathy. Late in his life I went to Halifax to meet him, and spoke with him through the mornings of a vividly remembered week; and I loved the man, as many others have done, as a teacher and as a kind of father and as an exemplar of integrity, wisdom, and moral beauty. I think he is among that small number — Leacock and Emily Carr come to mind — who had something to say to the whole world that could only be said by a Canadian.

Grant would declare that he was not a philosopher, and I have heard others sneeringly agree with this assessment. He was certainly not an academic philosopher, though he worked in universities most of his adult life. The pursuit of truth can never be a job description, and Grant was not immodest enough to give himself titles. But we are free to bestow titles upon him. To a remarkable degree, this man thought with his whole body and being, and suffered the pragmatism that is the sophistry of our age with a species of physical pain. When he came to public affairs, he came crashing into the greenhouse from the night outside. He did not belong in the world of politics, he did not know much about the hothouse life of party fund raising and late-night committee meetings, he did not often make it his business to know, and even when he did he was bored by it — for Grant was a philosopher, a man who loved wisdom and sought the truth, an enterprise in which the human individual will always fail, and fail badly, and must never give up. It is no surprise that such a man has naive things to say about economic planning and foreign policy. More than once, when I visited him, Grant said to me that if it had been his business to practise statecraft he would have made a study of the national debt, of military preparedness, of customs tariffs, of the regulation of Great Lakes Shipping, etc. He did not read newspapers carefully. Two public issues moved him sufficiently to make a stand, to come crashing into the greenhouse: the defeat of John Diefenbaker's government by the Liberals in 1963, and the toleration of abortion in the Omnibus Bill of 1969. There is not enough time in one life to do many things, and so Grant gave his attention to these two parochial issues (the latter having cost, in Canada alone, some hundreds of thousands of human lives by the time of Grant's death), and to the larger question of the fate of man in the modern world.

Philosophy is an exacting discipline in which you must earn your right to an opinion, but politics is a subject in which everyone has that right, and has both an opinion and a vote, down to the lowliest Zellers' shop clerk who cannot find Canada on a map of the world. It would be a terrible mistake to pass quickly over Grant's thinking on the highest matters to which the human mind may apply itself, and then take his casual and sometimes contradictory pronouncements on mundane issues as an oracle. Yet this inevitably happens whenever Grant's politics are discussed by people who have a very slight interest in philosophy and a very big interest in public affairs. Such an approach is effectively encouraged in the humane departments of the modern university, where classical learning is displaced more and more by the so-called "social sciences," so that even the study of history degenerates into half-baked sociological speculation. In such an environment the greatest men and women are in little danger of being understood. They are simply placed on a wall-chart, in a game of pin-the-tail-on-the-donkey with partially examined vogue labels.

Even when dealing with the limited question of Grant's view of Canadian nationality, we must acknowledge the breadth of this subject and its historical depth. The Canada to which Grant refers is not the Canada in the morning's *Globe and Mail*. It has two founding peoples: one of them shot pre-modern roots right into the soil of North America, and grew through four centuries into a great sturdy oak until recently it was sawn down for plywood. The other was the loser of that revolutionary war in which the spirit of Liberty first burst its chains. The French Canadian nation is transfigured in the mediaeval myth of Saint John the Baptist, who was carried in his mother's womb to a wise old age; the English Canadian nation is descended from the first people to be tarred and feathered in the name of the Rights of Man.

II

A second point, when discussing Grant's view of Canada, is that he only wrote directly on this matter in the former of two distinct phases of his life as a thinker. By dividing his writings into two groups, I do not mean to contradict the analysis in the best available study of Grant's thought, *George Grant and the Twilight of Justice*, by Joan O'Donovan; I only mean to merge the first two of the three phases she has discerned. The distinction I would draw is between the younger Grant, an inspired schoolteacher and fighting patriot, progressively disengaging himself from illusions about the modern world; and the other Grant, who wants serenity without illusions. I think the earlier phase is a continuous development from *The Empire: Yes or No?* through *Philosophy in the Mass Age* and *Lament for a Nation* to something like a mature statement in the essays of *Technology and Empire*. The later phase is evident from *English-Speaking Justice*. There is no fixed temporal boundary between these phases, and indeed the older Grant is antici- pated in 1945, and the younger Grant resurfaces occasionally in later life, especially in interviews and short articles where he is being asked to repeat himself. But between these phases I discern a change of mood, which I attribute to a deeper Christianity. Grant has two distinct ways of looking at politics, corresponding to these phases. The younger Grant involves himself with all aspects of the Canadian identity, and flirts with (though he is never seduced by) political

61

prescriptions; the older Grant involves himself politically in little more than the abortion controversy, and seems to be guided by the maxim Thomas More shouted from the scaffold: "When you can't make the good happen, prevent the very worst from happening."

We are really discussing one book, *Lament for a Nation*, published in 1965 and read by almost every intelligent person in Canada — some thousands of people. It is a Canadian contribution to a peculiarly twentieth-century genre, the short pessimistic tract that conveys a political outlook through a sensibility. I will name two other famous examples: *Notes Towards the Definition of Culture* by T.S. Eliot, and *The Revolt of the Masses* by Ortega y Gasset. These are books which cry out to be a formative influence on young people in college. By this I don't mean to condemn them, for each has had a formative influence on me; they are points of departure, not points of arrival, and they will be taken as departure by a lively mind. The *Lament* will be a formative book so long as there is a political entity called Canada, it will tend to immortalize the occasion from which it sprang, and it will be read differently by different generations. It will find readers largely because of its literary qualities, but they will respond to it with the exhilaration of the discovered idea.

In *Lament for a Nation* Grant bewailed the loss of Canada as if he were watching the city neighbourhood he had grown up being laid waste by developers; but as the camera backs up we see that Canada is part of a larger loss, that in the whole project of modernity, the idea of Canada is unsustainable. Among both French and English, though divergent confessionally, linguistically, historically, and culturally, there had been a sense of social order, of hierarchy and continuity, founded in a public conception of virtue as opposed to private conceptions of life, liberty, and the pursuit of happiness. Both communities could be content with the constitutional arrangements of 1791, and with later elaborations, which granted a wider authority to Church and State than would be contemplated in the United States. Both feared the extinction of community which seemed a corollary of the libertarian ideas so loudly and deceitfully expressed in Jefferson's Declaration of Independence, and inextricably embedded in the American Constitution. Neither quite grasped the heady implications of these documents: that "life" means youth, that "liberty" means pleasure, and that "the pursuit of happiness" means getting rich.

The *Lament* is a wonderfully sustained, remorseless, sharp, irresistible polemic that reminds one in its intuitive strokes of Ruskin, Blake, Marx, Demosthenes, and the prophet Isaiah in the King James Version. It is a righteous book, and this is its most extraordinary literary accomplishment; for who today can declaim righteously without tripping into self-righteousness again and again? It does sometimes trip — especially in the last chapter that begins, "Perhaps we should rejoice in the disappearance of Canada"[1] — into a kind of noble sulking so that the reader loses the thread of drama and becomes conscious of a pose: but it is an attractive and human pose for all that.

It is an explicitly anti-American book, for the developers of the metaphor speak with a Yankee accent, although ultimately they are just developers and any accent they have must be an historical accident. Grant's anti-Americanism, which came to the surface over matters like the war in Vietnam (about which I think he was seriously misinformed), is genuinely rooted in the old loyalism, the stuff that gave English Canada the only identity that it can ever have. In the hands of Grant, or Leacock, or John A. Macdonald, the old loyalism becomes a powerful and interesting force: not a second-best to the rhetoric and ideals of the American Revolution, but something deeper. The old image of mill and church in the clearing, symbolizing the efforts of our ancestors to harness the wilderness of nature and the wilderness in the heart of man, lurks behind the trolling phrases, though it is never explicitly mentioned; and behind that the flickering memory of tar and feathers, the payment many of our ancestors received for their defence of God, King, and Country. Grant was still a Loyalist, and I am still a Loyalist, and so is everyone in whose breast the heart of Loyalty is beating, whether his fathers were English, or Hong Kong Chinese — for loyalism is an affair of both the head and the heart, and "it doesn't mean a thing unless it has that swing." As a literary document, *Lament for a Nation* delivers the force of Grant's British North American sensibility, founded in loyalty, out of the domain of philosophy and into the glasshouse of our civic life.

In an important way the book presents a problem, largely created by its literary excellence. His later books are more cautious. Gerald Owen, who like me considers himself something of a disciple of Grant, has described the *Lament* as "perhaps the greatest crank letter of our time," and I would like to entertain this judgment for a moment.

While the book triumphantly conveys a political attitude, its substance is history, and its history is largely contemporary and partial. Yet unlike a Hooker, a Clarendon, or a Burke, who also wrote history that was contemporary and partial, Grant writes without the knowledge of a participant, and is at pains to remain an outsider. The characters in the book — Diefenbaker, Green, Pearson, Howe, Duplessis, Roosevelt, Kennedy — are too much like their stereotypes in contemporary newspapers. Grant says that their motives are unnecessary to his argument, but you cannot write history, including contemporary history, without coming to terms with individual psychologies, and Grant cannot avoid writing some kind of history. It is the younger Grant who is in the power of Hegel, and writes what appears sometimes to be a vignette from a philosophy of history.

This is not the place, and I am not the person, to discuss Hegel; but to elucidate the problem I find in *Lament for a Nation* I must state my prejudice baldly. I do not think it is given to men to write a philosophy of history, any more than it is given to us to write a treatise on the hierarchy of the angels. We can argue that history must have a meaning, or that the angels must exist, but this is about as far as we can take either inquiry short of revelation. It is Hegel's pantheism that I most fear, his confidence that we can grasp the mechanism of history from the parts that are presented. Quite possibly Hegel's pantheism is compensated for by his idealism, for he does not locate the "end of history" in historical time; but we know what carnage has been wreaked by the Hegelians.

Yet what Grant has to say about technology finally casts free of any determinism. The history behind *Technology and Empire* is that of the real eighteenth century — when a particular conception of human liberty was hatched (in minds such as Rousseau's) without a profound counterbalancing conception of human tyranny; it was a time of remarkable technical inventiveness, including the intellectual production that matures in Adam Smith's *Wealth of Nations*. The combination of that emancipation, with that naivete, with that material capability, was the Frankenstein that staggers through modern life and which Grant calls technology. Towards the close of this earlier phase of his thought he sets himself to think this monster, even to think what good it has done — for in the end it has fed, clothed, and housed us, and given us a taste of freedom that we can never go back on.

But I am wandering into what George Grant would have said are very deep waters. The danger I see in *Lament for a Nation*, as a history without individual motives, is that it loiters at the precipice of historical simplicities; and Grant is sometimes guilty of an almost Marxian imprecision, where social, cultural, ecclesiastical, economic, military, administrative, and political agencies are intertwined to make a very thick rope. It is a deeply sincere book, and therefore a book to be read carefully. When I spoke to him twenty years later about its reception, Grant regretted that only a handful of readers had got the point, and that most had got it backwards — reading *Lament* as a call to action, specifically as a call to socialist action to close the stable door now that the horse was gone. Grant's lament was for the horse, not for the straw it left in the stable.

III

The *Lament* was published in 1965. It would be a mistake to read it anachronistically, in terms of the nationalist movement that took shape in Canada in the late sixties, and which has given us Margaret Atwood as its most talented figure. The textbook of the literary wing of this movement — and it was largely a movement of one wing — was her *Survival*, published in the next decade. Atwood conveys to the handsomely-subsidized new "CanLit" programmes a sense of the Canadian as inevitable victim, as an oppressed colonial whose voice rises to join the choir of all the wretched of the earth, and whose yearning for emancipation is adequately described in the vocabulary of international feminism, along with various themes and characters that may be taken as typically Canadian. The book was ingeniously applied to the temper of its moment, a time when the Liberals had succeeded in stripping away almost all the outward symbols and decorations of our traditional national life, and when the young needed something to replace them. It was a conception of Canada that would have been meaningless to most of the historical figures that Atwood presents as components in her new curriculum — especially those who wrote in English, who did not think of themselves as a colonized people but rather as colonizers and civilizers of the New

World. The implied equation of British with American colonialism is just what Grant was always fighting.

I am being harsh with Atwood, and I do not wish to be gratuitously so, for I think she is a very fine artist. Her successes in New York and London awaken in me a quite involuntary Canadian pride, and I only protest that she weakens that talent, and divides that exquisite, excruciating energy, by her frequent descents into cultural politics, where the cutting precision of her poems and the rich, almost nostalgic particularity of her novels must be replaced by mnemonic slogans and formulae.

There are two big problems with the variety of nationalism that I am associating with *Survival*. The first is that it is false; it does not make terms with the actual Canada that Grant recalled to life in *Lament for a Nation*, it does not offer continuity. The second is that, whether or not it is false, it is reductive: it introduces arbitrary, extra-literary standards that can only be criteria for what to throw away.

Here a digression is needed, because reductionism is not the peculiar fault of Margaret Atwood. I am not using Grant's terminology, but I think I am in company with him when I say that the hideousness of technology is that it is reductive, that it levels, that it has levelled even the Protestant culture that provided its first patrons. It does not seek to include, but to exclude — to eliminate the redundant rather than to assimilate the good. In Hobbes and Locke, in Hume and Dewey we find a deadly reversal of the spirit that animated Albert the Great and Thomas Aquinas in the High Middle Ages (and which comes down to us in a failed English tradition through Richard Hooker). Instead of the stimulating aliveness of the thirteenth century -which embraces Aristotle from the moment he is recovered, and ransacks the Arabians for glimmerings of truth; which eagerly reconstructs its own edifice to include everything of worth in the new learning, while endlessly testing the foundations — we have a spirit that is constantly ransacking itself.

We have what I like to call the "spirit of jar-placement," from a poem by Wallace Stevens:

> I placed a jar in Tennessee,
> And round it was, upon a hill.
> It made the slovenly wilderness
> Surround that hill.

Our modern philosophers (and here I am indulging the same spirit of jar-placement) never stop looking for a skeleton key that will unlock everything and replace God; in political terms, a jar to place upon a hill, that will bring the surrounding wilderness to heel if not to order. You find this in Marx, Darwin, Freud: the daring presentation of the single insight. And once our moderns think they have found their key, they, or their followers, discard all their other possessions. They may find it at either extreme of a great number of polar opposites — in anarchy one day, and in tyranny the next — but in a variation upon the myth of Sisyphus, they seem doomed to return perpetually to the lost-and-found.

When I say "reductionism" I mean to communicate my belief in the unending futility of this modern quest, this project to decide what is important so that we can throw everything else away. Like Grant, I suspect that God is the answer; that, to put it crudely, until God is put back in his heaven, for all to see, we will not be able to put the lesser things of this world in anything resembling a just order, a hierarchy of greater and lesser goods. Like Grant's, I suppose, my political and social instincts want a place for everybody and everbody in his place, not the "one size fits all" of modern liberalism.

Here again I have strayed into deep waters, and at my back I hear George Grant's whistle blowing like a lifeguard's. The more limited point is that Atwood's nationalism is nationalist without being patriotic. It tends less to the evocation of a tradition and a geography than to the enunciation of a party line. It associates Canada with a single view of itself, and it sets us up to make passionless, almost automated, invidious comparisons between the present-day Canada and the present-day United States — something Grant only did when he was angry. It redefines Canada in cosmopolitan terms, through this promiscuous use of feminist vocabulary, as if the struggle to preserve Canadian independence were somehow a local front in the international struggle for the emancipation of women. It has contributed to an unfortunate reductive effect, for even today it is difficult to get a hearing in the Ontario media without first tipping your hat to several nationalist and feminist cliches. (To be fair I can't blame Atwood for this, it is the work of people considerably shallower than herself.)

Grant's patriotic nationalism looks backward, not forward (with the exception of the remarkable passage in Chapter 6, where he correctly predicts that when Catholicism disintegrates in Quebec it will be like a dam bursting, and all the clever young people will rush out to embrace American-style entrepreneurship with a vengeance).[2] It looks backward because that is the only attractive prospect. We cannot make sense of the *Lament* by reading it as a pioneering contribution to the deracinated nationalism of the seventies, the sort of nationalism that could be patronized by Pierre Trudeau, and which was anyway extinguished in the free trade election.

In this and other ways, Grant must be protected from his friends. I shall give two more examples, one general and one particular: both of people Grant told me he very much liked and admired, and both associated with Grant's "message" in the minds of Canadian nationalists.

The general example is Dennis Lee, who among other ministrations I believe provided Grant with the useful services of an editor. Grant and Lee formed a mutual admiration based at least partly on a fascination with each other's first premises. They knew they disagreed about the most important things. It is a wonderful characteristic of real friendship that the most important things don't get in the way: my own best friend in the world is an uncompromising Scottish atheist. William F. Buckley and John Kenneth Galbraith are buddies. We have to grasp from a distance what Grant and Lee knew at first hand: that friends are not necessarily allies.

The particular example is Gad Horowitz, whose helpful suggestion that Grant was a "red tory" has led to more confusion about the meanings of those words than any Canadian oxymoron since John Bracken's "Progressive Conservative." Almost anyone who questions the precedence given in North America to liberty over social order is, after the presentation of this identity tag, likely to be rolled into a red blanket that will be tied at both ends; certainly it has this effect on Grant. What stands behind the tag is Horowitz's assertion that "socialism has more in common with Toryism than with liberalism, for liberalism is possessive individualism, which socialism and Toryism are variants of collectivism."[3] Now, this is half true, and as Stephen Leacock said, the advantage of a half-brick over a whole one in an argument is that it carries farther. At the root of toryism is an intuition that liberty is meaningless without social order and social definition;

that in this sense order is prior to liberty, and the liberty of the individual must be in many ways curtailed, or given context. Grant certainly thought this way, and spoke of himself in conversation as a tory. But somebody should have asked Grant if he agreed that toryism is a variant of collectivism. The statement is not even plausible.

The man who quoted Hooker with such warmth at the front of the *Lament* is not a Red. He is a straight-shooting, dyed in the wool, navy-blue Tory; or red in the old sense, for red was once the standard of the Tory party, before the colour came to be associated in the Tory mind with the murk of blood spilled in revolutionary gutters. For Grant socialism meant a railway to the Pacific, a power grid in Ontario, and the CBC — things which fall some miles short of socialism. He was glad to call himself a socialist if it would make his listener happy, in the same way the Buddhist folk of upcountry Thailand say they are Christians, in order to keep the missionaries off their backs. (The first law of polite society is that flattery buys silence.) I don't know whether or not Grant realized that in Canada, since the demise of the old Co-operative Commonwealth Federation, socialism has been offered not as a means of preserving our community identity, but as an alternative to it — to make Canada less like the United States by making it more like Albania.

In print, in his contributions to secular debate, the term Grant favoured was "conservative." Unfortunately this word is ambiguous, for it may refer to anybody from a mild Tory to an old Bolshevik to a libertarian who wants to sell heroin in vending machines. It is a word which we associate in English-speaking politics with Edmund Burke, to suggest the re-articulation of the old Whig *and* Tory positions in reaction to the carnage in France.

I have tried to think through the usage of the terms "Tory" and "Conservative" in an absolute sense, because I am often vexed by the casual use of them. I think we should agree to something like these definitions: (1) Toryism is the political expression of a religious view of life. (2) Conservatism is an attempt to maintain Toryism after you have lost your faith. (3) Progressive Conservatism is an attempt to maintain conservatism after you have lost your memory, too. Put another way, conservatism is just Toryism after a haemorrhage; or Toryism in a passive, modest, self-conscious, unsatisfying, and self-defeating form.

In this sense, Grant was a Tory. At the end of the day, he was less curious about how we should administer the hospital insurance plan or the egg marketing board, than about what kind of civilization we have created.

IV

I think a Canadian patriotic nationalism should concern itself, can only concern itself at this point, with the hopeful preservation of the surviving Canadian institutions — hopeful in the sense that another generation may find a use for them. If I may make a short inventory of what we have left, out of the fairly extensive inheritance of our fathers, I would start with Crown-in-Parliament. More than anything in the attic, this is what distinguishes us from the Republicans to the south: the essentially unicameral nature of our (ceremonially bicameral) parliament. Together with the preservation of party discipline, this institution gives the government of the day some chance of standing up to external pressures; of acting when necessary, and of not acting when action would be counter-productive. Proposals for senate reform from the west would vitiate the House of Commons by subjecting it to competition with an elected Senate.

Neither do I think our parliamentary system can survive the loss of its greatest external symbol of legitimacy: the monarch. Getting rid of this apparently redundant decorative flourish would be like stripping Parliament Hill of the Peace Tower because you don't like the sound of bells. The truth is I am not sure if we still have a monarch, for one can only judge from the sides of the mail vans, and from the fact that the Governor-General has gone around calling herself the Head of State, which she most certainly is not under the Canadian constitution. I take no comfort in her retirement; voices should have been raised for her removal.

After Trudeau's Charter of Rights and Freedoms I am not sure there is much left to defend in the system of Common Law, which gave us the world's most successful bulwark against tyranny. Trudeau, whatever he thought he was doing, replaced a sound, working system of legal precedent and experience (infinitely preferable to the judicial circuses in the United States) with an American-style tissue of promises, negotiated under the glare of klieg lights among an exceptionally moronic batch of provincial premiers. With Trudeau you could never tell what was done on principle and what for spite; but whichever the motive the destruction was appalling. There is the same confusion of motives in Ian Scott's proposals for court reform, now before the Ontario legislature. The only purpose they can serve, besides demoralizing the Ontario judiciary, is to destroy the distinction that can be made between homicide and parking tickets.

Generally, our only hope in the realm of law is that, by some miracle of divine grace, the next generation of judges will not try to use the powers the Charter is begging them to use. Certainly the present legal trend, which goes beyond accepting the claims of individual liberty over social order, to accepting the claims of economic equality over individual liberty, has been encouraged by the Charter, and can only end badly.

Our social welfare system, celebrated as if it were a pillar of our national identity, is, despite hysterical assertions, only marginally better than that of the United States. It is threatened not by the extraordinary wickedness of Cabinet ministers, but by the size of the national debt. Almost everyone, including everyone in Cabinet, agrees that the system ought to be preserved as fully as possible; but it will not be preserved by demagogic posturing.

The preservation of the civility of Canadian streets, relative to the zoo-like atmosphere of American inner cities, probably depends most on the government's present willingness to co-operate with the United States authorities in the interception of drug shipments from Latin America.

As for free trade in the less harmful goods and services, I don't think anything can be gained by trying to resist the international trend towards freer access to markets, and therefore towards broader commercial competition in all those products which have no national or cultural or aesthetic significance whatever. It should be clear by now that the opponents of free trade offer nothing better than a way to make us poorer as an end in itself. Prosperity is a good, and I don't want us to become a nation of smugglers. Moreover, I know at first hand what happens to manufacturing standards when our businessmen are protected by punitive import duties. I don't want a Canada that is associated with shoddy goods and petty bureaucratic restrictions.

Anti-Americanism is a problem in itself, though more for our souls than for any practical consequence of our incessant national whining. Since about 1865, I can't see that the Americans have done anything to earn our especial resentment of them. As a people they are conspicuously more generous than we are. It is a bit late to hold them responsible for the evils of their constitution, and we might show some sympathy as they try to make the best of it. We are most shrill when accusing them of faults that we share. The greatest irritant seems to be their immense size, which again they cannot help. It is embarrassing to visit the United States, and hear how well they wish us; to hear, moreover, that the fate of modern man is also their fate -that they are uncertain about their identities, and mad as this must sound, sometimes look to Canada for suggestions. That they can be thoughtlessly patronizing towards us I don't deny; but then the Poles do the same to the Lithuanians — it is a function of big and small. We should be glad that they are not trying to kill us, and get on with it.

Perhaps we should rejoice in the disappearance of Canada, since it gives us an advantage in the contemporary West, where nationalism has been discredited for good reasons. As a nation Canada has been relatively harmless, and we might hope to perish without much blood on our hands. The idea of the nation-state is surprisingly recent, and on balance it hasn't worked out. It seems singularly unfitted for a world that has broader cosmopolitan horizons, and narrower cultural components. I often think Toronto is too large to be a nation, and Canada is too small. Some new arrangement, encompassing vast empire and tiny city states, may emerge from the pressure of circumstance, and Canada will become like Dacia, a patch of colour in an historical atlas — restored to the pink of the British empire in the telescoping of time. Our children might still live here, and that part of us which is rooted could still be passed down through the generations.

But these points are removing to a great distance; I have strayed far from shore, so that I can't even see Grant anymore, and must try to remember where he is. Where do we go from here? How do we find a place for the Good in the midst of the world that is around us, on anything larger than an individual scale? I cannot answer such questions, and I am not being facetious when I say that they are terribly difficult, and that the only answer I can give to Grant's shade is that I am thinking hard about them, and feeling lost without him.

NOTES

1   George Grant, *Lament for a Nation — The Defeat of Canadian Nationalism.*
     (Ottawa: Carleton University Press, 1989), p. 88.

2   Ibid., p. 80.

3   Gad Horowitz, "Conservatism, Liberalism, and Socialism: An Inter-
     pretation," *The Canadian Journal of Economic and Political Science,*
     XXXII, no.2 (Toronto: University of Toronto Press, May 1966), p. 168.

COMMENTARY

Gad Horowitz

Kim Campbell, Member of Parliament for Vancouver Centre and currently Minister of State for Indian Affairs and Northern Development in the Mulroney government, prepared herself for this session by "hastily reviewing" *Lament for a Nation*, and found herself in a "rage" at its "quintessentially central Canadian" British Imperialist outlook, which has assigned to the western provinces the role of "hewers of wood and drawers of water." "The conception of Canada," she suggests, "that is lamented by George Grant and others, is a Canada whose history is a colonial history... a history in which central Canada has arrogated to itself the right to define what the roles of the components of this country will be." Intoning against the tariff policy, which, as she sees it, prevented the development of industry in British Columbia, and resulted in a hidden transfer of wealth from the West to Ontario and Quebec, Ms. Campbell rejected the sentiment "that laments the loss of a national conception which planted the seeds that now are flowering and that most threaten the continuance of the nation to which I am committed." The Free Trade Agreement, the argument goes, reverses this centralist bias. The opening of markets with the United States, she claimed, is essential for the development of economic diversification in western Canada; Grant's concept of a nation, which depends upon the subjugation of the Atlantic and western regions, is obsolete now that the Conservative party is no longer controlled by central Canada. The political ascendancy of the Conservatives has also made possible a reversal of the traditionally divisive handling of the Quebec question; the Conservatives will overcome the tragic "anti-Quebec sentiment in the West, which has the potential to be so destructive to our national integrity, and which is a direct result of economic nationalism practised in the interests of central Canada." For British Columbia, she maintained, the point of a revised nationalism that does not build on the concept of a nation relying on the subjugation of the regions is to attain a competitive edge internationally:

> We want to compete in the markets of the Pacific and we cannot compete against Taiwan, Hong Kong, Korea, and Singapore — or even India — unless we have the efficiency that comes from competition in a large market. The Free Trade Agreement, which will make it possible to develop valued-added industry in British Columbia's primary resources, is the key to that development.

Ms. Campbell also minimized the contemporary importance of Canada's British past: "The coming of British parliamentary democracy to Canada was a very important development, but it is no more important than the arrival of William the Conqueror in England in 1066 or the Glorious Revolution in 1688." Canada's historic continuity begins well before the coming of the British: "When Stonehenge was being built there had been people living in my part of the world for thousands of years ....the British are sort of 'jumped up' newcomers." "And perhaps," she repeated, "we ought to start thinking of our country in those terms and understand that we do have roots, that we do have a long history, that we do have a sense of identity ... which goes back thousands of years." British institutions, yes, but these were grafted onto indigenous practices.

So much for the party of John A. Macdonald and John Diefenbaker.

The approaches of the next two panelists were very different from Campbell's. Picking up on the central theme of David Warren's paper, they seemed determined to save the image of George Grant from too close an identification with "narrow" Canadian nationalism, and socialism. In company with Warren's "Zeller's shop clerk" who "cannot find Canada on a map of the world," Dennis Lee, Margaret Atwood, Mel Hurtig, Gad Horowitz, and other simple-minded leftists and feminists might want to take seriously, literally, and straighforwardly some of the message of *Lament*: that there is something deeply wrong not simply with "modernity," but with the capitalist economic system, the system of organized greed which in both its "private" and statist forms, overwhelms the human spirit with its technological conquest of nature; that Canada's capitalist elites have been selling out this country; that the fight for Canadian independence from the United States, though many of us sometimes feel that it is doomed to defeat, and though it does not solve the deepest problems of Canada as a part of the modern world, is a worthwhile project, worthy of admiration and critical support. Warren, Ajzenstat and Forbes, while not denying the presence of these themes in *Lament*, all urged in different ways that they not be taken too seriously, as either valid in themselves or as expressions of the true depth of Grant's thought.

Warren pointed out that Grant's views on "economic planning" and foreign policy matters "like the war in Vietnam," were "naive," "casual and sometimes contradictory," "seriously misinformed," "guilty of an almost Marxian imprecision." As a profound conservative thinker rather than a practical man of the political world Grant should be forgiven for these small errors, not lumped in with Lee, Atwood, Horowitz and others. Grant himself had told Warren that *Lament* ought not to have been taken "as a call to action, specifically as a call to socialist action." However, Warren and perhaps Grant himself misinterpreted our reading of *Lament*. We never did take it as a call to action. In my review of *Lament* ("Tories, Socialists and the Demise of Canada," *Canadian Dimension*, May-June 1965) I strongly criticized Grant precisely for his failure to call for action. In spite of Warren's assertion that Grant's backward-looking nationalism "obviously" cannot be read as a "pioneering contribution" to our forward-looking nationalism, we were encouraged in our nationalist and socialist projects by Grant's work. He did not repudiate us for that in those days, nor do I believe he would have done so now.

Warren vociferously denies that there is any shred of validity in my suggestion that Grant was a red Tory. The "intuition that ... social order is prior to liberty" is simply good old "navy-blue" Toryism; there is nothing red about it. If the prioritization of social order were the sole constituent of Grant's political thought, I would have to agree with Warren. The priority of the community, or "collectivism," is a concept that Toryism and socialism have in common, but it does not make Toryism red. It is necessary to go farther, as Grant did, towards the specifically socialist idea: the critique and condemnation of economic inequality as oppressive and exploitative of the common people. The argument that looking backward cannot be taken as a contribution to those who also want to look forward, is a *non sequitur*. Christian socialism looks backward to Isaiah and Jesus, and forward to socialism. Was there no affinity between socialism and the argument of Grant's beautiful essay, "An Ethic for Community," published in *Social Purpose for Canada*, the book that inaugurated the New Democratic Party on the Canadian intellectual scene and which was edited by Michael Oliver, first president of the NDP? "The end which any society should be working for," Grant wrote,

> is the elimination of ... relations of superiority and subordination in all aspects of life.... my duty to regard persons [as equal] is a duty higher than my valuing of the true, the noble, or the beautiful.... the hierarchy of talents must always be subordinate ... to the basic equality of persons.... It is often argued that by maintaining a wealthy and privileged class certain 'finer things' are kept alive. What are these 'finer things' that owe their survival to the rich, and which would not continue in a more egalitarian society? ... What noble culture is the product of Forest Hill and Westmount which might be threatened by greater equality?[1]

How many "navy blue" tories or Straussians have written lines like those?

Grant never repudiated his critique of capitalist inequality. Even the older, more conservative Grant became a close student and admirer of Simone Weil. Is there no affinity between Weil and socialism?

During the sixties Grant worked very closely with people on the new left. His consistently fierce opposition to the American Empire and its war on Vietnam was not rooted exclusively in his loyalism and his love of traditional cultures. His praise for Abbie Hoffman and Jerry Rubin was not simply the forgivable eccentricity of a cantankerous navy-blue Tory.

During the sixties there was a real alliance between a number of red Tories, including Grant, on the one hand, and a number of left-wing nationalists, anarchists, and socialists on the other. Such an alliance must seem absurd to conservatives of the Mulroney era. It needs to be repressed. Warren fills the need.

Janet Ajzenstat's contribution focused not on the *Lament* but on my argument in "Conservatism, Liberalism and Socialism in Canada" (*Canadian Journal of Economic and Political Science*, 1966) that Canada has been less liberal and individualistic than the United States. She argues that doubts have recently been raised about the position of those American scholars who question the view that Americans neglected the "importance of public virtue" and "religion" in favour of "crass self-interest" as the foundation of their regime. And Canadian scholars such as Peter J. Smith and Gordon Stewart are putting forward a new view of the Loyalists as "the champions of an individualist ideology... only too willing to sacrifice the common good to party and career." She suggested that George Grant is now being enlisted by "the new school, this new interpretation of our Canadian past," as a thinker who represents, in individualistic Canada, the American tradition of "civic republicanism" or public virtue. She concludes that, given our mutable understanding of the difference between the foundations of the Canadian and American regimes, and given also that Grant had some good things to say about liberalism, we ought to follow David Warren in rejecting all "petty" attempts to enlist the deep thought of George Grant, his thought about the "good," for various causes in the name of Canadian nationalism.

In my view, Ajzenstat's contribution is so remarkable that it takes my breath away every time I think about it. I would like to comment on only one key point: the crucial difference between liberalism and collectivism is not about selfishness versus altruism. The dispute is not ethical but ontological. Liberalism sees society essentially as an association of radically autonomous individuals. This view is not at all incompatible, as Kant's teaching shows so very well, with devotion to duty. Only in an American language-game could individualism and civic republicanism become polarized. What makes civic republicanism anything more than the bad conscience of liberalism? Collectivism is not simply the assertion of the importance of public virtue as opposed to crass self-interest. It sees the individual essentially as a member of the organic community.

As for the new view of the Loyalists, Tory ideologies can be personally selfish; liberal ideologies can be personally self-sacrificing.

Proponents of public virtue and religion can be individualists. Margaret Thatcher, no Tory, but surely a devotee of public virtue, has said: "There is no such thing as society." American individualism has, since its Puritan beginnings, been more religious and more public-spirited, less "radical" than European individualism. The best discussion of this is the first chapter of Louis Hartz's great work on the Liberal Tradition (*sic*) in America.

Don Forbes joins with Warren as well, announcing his agreement that "what is most striking ... and most quotable" in the *Lament* has little to do with "the heart of the argument." The heart of the argument is the expression of concern for the fate of "purposes for man higher than the expression of human freedom in the conquest of nature." The *Lament* ought not to be taken as a practical warning but as "a point of departure" for philosophical "reflection" about "the principles by which we live" in modernity. Our problem is how to think about the good in the contemporary context.

The text of the *Lament*, Forbes pointed out, supports two separate interpretations: either it's about "building social democracy" in Canada or it's about "the British tradition and British conservatism." He admits that "these two things are not entirely unrelated and are both important." However many people err in "paying too much attention to social democracy and insufficient attention to the British connection." Readers like Mel Hurtig take the *Lament*, Forbes maintains, and visualize "at the end an aroused national sentiment in Canada expressed through marches in the streets, the workers, the students, the teachers with their flags flying; and dismiss as misplaced and unimportant Grant's emphasis on the British connection and the British tradition." The main point of the *Lament*, says Forbes, is that "the dream of building a conservative nation rooted in the connection with Great Britain ... had always been just a dream." Forbes suggests that Grant had succeeded:

> ...in evoking the experience of an awakening from that
> dream, from that unreality of our politics at an earlier
> period without joining in the public celebration of
> what had replaced it of the forces or the aspirations that
> destroyed the dream. He succeeded in showing the
> readers ... what was involved in one area of great

concern to us as a people, as a nation, what it meant more formulaically to live critically in the dynamo.

The Americanization of Canada is "fated," inescapable", and not all bad. The only question now is: what can we, and all the other Americans in the world, from Inuvik to New York, to Warsaw, to Singapore, do now to protect the human spirit from materialism?

My comments on Warren apply also to Forbes. The only difference between them is Forbes' more nuanced position on Grant's connection with socialism. The relationship between the British conservative tradition and the Canadian social gospel/social democratic tradition is admitted — only to be dismissed. The struggle to preserve Canadian social democracy and Canadian sovereignty is vulgar and unworthy. Grant's admiration for the Quebecois' determination to go down "with guns blazing" is ignored, or downplayed and forgiven. At the bottom line Forbes tells us that Grant's "major contribution" — his call for deep thought about the good — "should not be lost in a quarrel about his practical politics."

Rainer Knopff was the only panelist who, without at all downplaying Grant's affinity with the left, was able to identify precisely his view of the essential difference between his own red Toryism and modern Canadian socialism: the left, like Toryism, looks back to "practical examples of ... wholeness" which it prefers to the "alienation of modern liberal life." However, as a movement of modern thought, the left proclaims "the artificiality of political order." It has abandoned "altogether" the idea that there is a law which subjects to normative limits the human will to mastery over nature. Grant admired "nationalism, Marxism, and the new left" for harkening "back to pre-modern practice," as "expressions of permanent human needs." But he rejected them insofar as they express "these needs from within a perspective which then denies that there are any permanent human needs." Thus, true needs are "distorted and turned into purposes of modernity." For example, nationalism, while it admirably expresses the patriotic impulse to preserve the traditions of a people, does so in such a manner as to become "a modernizing and homogenizing force."

The problem with Grant's position (which is, I assume, shared by Knopff) is that it wrongly attributes to all leftist thought a total historicization of nature. We are not all Nietzscheans, any more than all conservatives are guilty of the naturalization of historically contingent institutions such as class domination and imperialism. We do not hear the Logos in the same way that conservatives do, but we are not deaf. They equate their version of the law with law *per se*, accusing us of antinomian devotion to praxis without concern for any standards of justice and virtue. This charge is false. In Marcuse's thought, for example, Eros does not destroy truth; rather, Marcuse "redefines it in his own terms."

The conservative rhetoric of "virtue" ignores the price that was paid in pre-modern societies for their version of unalienated wholeness. I am thinking of the exclusion of virtually the entire population from participation in learning, power, security, and dignity. For them there was never much more than the teaching, as Edmund Burke put it, of their "consolation in the final proportions of eternal justice." It is my impression that George Grant remained to the end of his life one of the very few conservatives who genuinely respected the demand of "ordinary" people for full inclusion in the community.

NOTES

[1]   George Grant, "An Ethic for Community," in Michael Oliver (ed.), *Social Purpose for Canada*. (Toronto: University of Toronto Press, 1961), p. 25.

GEORGE GRANT
AND THE LEGACY OF LAMENT FOR A NATION

Andrew Stark

In *Lament for a Nation*, the three great "modern political theories" — liberalism, conservatism, and Marxism — are each shown to have stolen one another's thunder in a particular way. In liberalism, Grant discerned a dynamic which leads ineluctably to "universality," "homogeneity" and thence to "tyranny." In conservatism — particularly of the American variety — Grant saw nothing so much as a cipher which takes its character from the historically-prior, bedrock Lockian liberalism it seeks to preserve (conservatives, he writes, "are old-fashioned liberals").[1] And in Marxism—and in socialism more broadly—Grant identified the only ideology which today propounds the conservative idea of order. Liberalism lies a hair's breadth from tyranny; conservatism is but a trustee for liberalism; Marxism (or "socialism"— in *Lament*, Grant uses the terms interchangeably) is the sole contemporary incarnation of conservative principles. It is only in the context of this paradoxical set of ideological understandings that one can consider Grant's legacy — or at least, at the legacy of *Lament for a Nation*.

First, though, one must consider what is meant by "the legacy of George Grant and *Lament for a Nation*." For participants, the central (though not the only) question of Grant's legacy had to do with the nature and extent of Grant's affection for socialism. Gad Horowitz argued that it was substantial. David Warren claimed that it was sharply delimited. Don Forbes suggested that a true measure could be taken only if Grant's affinity with socialism is weighed against his anglophilia. Rainer Knopff balanced it against his antiquarianism. Most, though, directly or indirectly asked the question: where did Grant, and in particular, the Grant of *Lament*, stand on socialism broadly conceived ?

The panelists considered the legacy of Grant and of *Lament* largely through the lenses of the 1988 free trade election. True, Janet Ajzenstat cautioned that "it is petty to enlist Grant for ideological reasons," and Don Forbes noted that "people with very different political positions can find inspiration in ... *Lament for a Nation.*" Their comments remind us that *Lament* is considerably more than an indication of the extent of Grant's socialism, or of his possible verdict on the Free Trade Agreement. Yet despite these reminders, the temptation to ask where the author of *Lament* might have stood in the 1988 campaign was very strong among the speakers and panelists. Of course, this is not the same as asking whether the "older George Grant" of the early 'eighties was, in fact, a proponent of free trade with the United States, nor, alternatively, whether the "younger George Grant" of *Lament* was pleased with Canada's particular economic arrangements with the United States in the mid-'sixties. These are the kinds of questions that might be labelled "anachronistic" or "acontextual" by intellectual historians, thought neither deserves the label, for each asks only what the George Grant of the time thought about the issues of the day. In doing so, they point up the difficulty with the main question, the question of Grant's legacy as it was understood in discussion: for asking what Grant as the author of *Lament* might have said about a political question that arose in a specific context a generation later, imposes on the book intellectual considerations and categories that would not have applied when the book was written; the question thus invites profound misreading of the text, even by those who might have known the "younger Grant" personally, and even though the "older Grant" survived to see the political issue in question emerge.

There is a sense, however, in which it is possible to ask where the Grant of *Lament* might have stood on the contemporary spectrum of left and right, and on the issue of the trade agreement in particular, without necessarily doing violence to Grant or to the book. When participants argue about whether Grant would have felt more at home among Ed Broadbent's New Democrats or Brian Mulroney's Progressive Conservatives, they illuminate not so much Grant's mind as their own. They do not examine authorial intention so much as reveal authorial influence. When Gad Horowitz suggests an alliance between the Grant of *Lament* and the contemporary Gad Horowitz, against the Tories and the free-traders, Horowitz is in large measure making a statement not about where Grant would have stood on the political issues of today, but about how Gad Horowitz and his political colleagues were influenced by — indeed, how they read — Grant and how they now use that reading to buttress their views. Horowitz himself underscores this point when he comments that, in a certain sense, "Grant himself misinterpreted our reading of *Lament*." Equally, in suggesting that Grant would have taken their part, David Warren, Mel Hurtig and others are saying as much about Grant's role in the formation of their own thought as they are about Grant's thought itself. Multiplied across readers, the enterprise of arguing Grant's likely position in the 1988 campaign affords a rough method of tracing and gauging the book's intellectual influence on the current debate and the current climate of political opinion. It may not be the most scientific contribution to the history of political ideas, but it may well mark the beginnings of an impressionistic political science.

Don Forbes suggested that, in examining the contemporary legacy of *Lament* "We're all called to think hard about ["the good in the contemporary context"] and the wonderful legacy that Grant has left us. . .is the assistance he gives us in thinking about that question." In other words, it is our thinking, as much as Grant's, that we explore when we ask about his legacy, about the relevance of his thoughts of a generation ago to the issues we face today. But in attempting to define Grant's legacy — in attempting to study the light shed by a reading of *Lament* on the value of various contemporary political complexions and dispositions, and on the FTA in particular — we must remember as Forbes says, that it is "a complex book," and what "is most striking in its argument and most quotable has to do with what seems to be the heart of its argument."

Mel Hurtig's reading of *Lament* illustrates Forbes' point. Hurtig was the only participant to discuss the early chapters on the 1963 campaign; in Hurtig's view, Grant saw Diefenbaker as an unapologetic and unreconstructed nationalist and Pearson as a sell-out. Hurtig's analysis points up what he sees as the Mulroney government's betrayal of Diefenbaker's nationalistic conservatism. Mulroney is certainly no Diefenbaker, but the Diefenbaker and Pearson of *Lament* both elude Hurtig's simplistic categorization. Grant's Diefenbaker emerges as a man possessed of a fourfold political psychology which results in a peculiarly stunted and troubled nationalism. Internationally, Grant's

Diefenbaker was motivated by a multilateralism which made him a partisan of — indeed, a stickler for — the autonomous instruments of international governance (the North Atlantic Treaty Organization in particular); this predisposition did, of course, serve the interests of Canadian foreign-policy independence. Beyond this, however, Diefenbaker's anti-communism and non-pacifism blinded him to any darker evils harboured in the imperialistic political culture of the American political elite; to the extent that he refused to "attack" American policy, he muted Canada's foreign-policy independence during his tenure. Domestically, by contrast, Diefenbaker's "prairie populism" made him sensible of the threat posed to independence by the continentalist political culture of the Ontario corporate elite. Thus, his prairie populism was compatible with a larger nationalism. But his "free enterprise" ideology made it impossible for him to be a partisan of — let alone a stickler for — the instruments of the national state; it blinded him to the fact that "only planning could restrain the victory of continentalism."[2] In the end, "The free enterprise assumptions of the Diefenbaker administration [Grant uses the American term 'administration' in place of the Canadian term 'government'] "...were obviously anti-national."[3] Hurtig, in contrasting Mulroney's Tories with Grant's Diefenbaker, cites Kenneth McNaught's remark that "genuine conservatives" were "prepared to use government. . .to limit private intrusions upon the public interest." But now, Hurtig adds, "a new generation of [Canadian] conservatives have abandoned a century of conservative traditions for their own variations of Reaganomics and Thatcherism." In so saying, Hurtig completely ignores Grant's manifold attacks on Diefenbaker for opposing controls on foreign investment, expanding the domain of private broadcasting at the expense of the Canadian Broadcasting Corporation, establishing the Glassco Commission, and generally refusing to use government to limit private intrusions on what Grant believed was the public interest.

For Grant, Diefenbaker's antipathy to the Ontario corporate elite and his steadfast support of multilateral institutions both served the cause of Canadian nationalism and independence; his antipathy to the institutions of the state, however, and his uncritical view of any criticism of the American governing elite, did not. Thus, Grant's Diefenbaker was outflanked internationally by Howard Green, who did "criticize American world policy," and domestically by Walter

Gordon, who was not afraid to use the state for nationalistic purposes. Diefenbaker's politics manifested a "limited nationalism": even, as Grant writes, an "anti-nationalism" — certainly not the unalloyed nationalism attributed to him by Hurtig.

Pearson and his Liberals, by contrast, are not the unrepentant sell-outs depicted by Hurtig. Grant writes that, in terms of their motives, nothing of what he says "implies that Pearson or ... Pickersgill, did not think of themselves as nationalists."[4] Moreover, they saw themselves as "realistic nationalists" who believed that building a nation "in terms of ... realities ... is not negating nationalism but recognizing its limits."[5] Not only was Pearson's nationalism inwardly pure and meant to be outwardly pragmatic, but it is also "perfectly convincing to argue that [his] policies were necessary ... [and] good for Canada"[6] — however ultimately unsuccessful they were in preserving Canadian sovereignty. When speaking of Diefenbaker's nationalism, Grant uses as basics such political concepts as the Ontario establishment, the American executive, the state, and multilateralism. But in speaking of Pearson's nationalism, he resorts to moral-philosophical concepts such as "intention," "realism," "necessity" and "good." Grant has deeper purposes here — purposes which escape Hurtig, who is looking in Grant for a simplistic portrayal of Diefenbaker as an unalloyed nationalist, in order to show how far the Mulroney Conservatives have fallen. In fact, Grant wants principally to show that at some deep level, Pearson's behaviour was beyond reproach, in order to demonstrate that lament is possible even in the face of necessity and goodness, even when Canada's disappearance is a "matter of necessity"[7] and might well "lead to some greater political good."[8]

Indeed, not only Diefenbaker and Pearson, but Grant himself is sometimes unrecognizable in Hurtig's rendition of *Lament*. To take just one example, Hurtig advises *en passant* that: "If you think about Meech Lake, think too about this from *Lament for a Nation*: 'The espousing by ... Canadian 'conservatives' of greater authority for [the provinces] has always had a phoney ring about it....'" The implication is that the author of *Lament* would have opposed Meech Lake. But if Hurtig insists on bringing *Lament* into the Meech Lake debate, he might also "think" about this:

> There was one aspect of Diefenbaker's nationalism that
> was repugnant to thoughtful French Canadians.... He

appealed to one united Canada, in which individuals would have equal rights irrespective of race and religion; there would be no first- and second-class citizens. As far as the civil rights of individuals are concerned, this is obviously an acceptable doctrine. Nevertheless, the rights of the individual do not encompass the rights of nations, liberal doctrine to the contrary. The French Canadians had entered Confederation not to protect the rights of the individual but the rights of a nation.... For Diefenbaker, the unity of all Canadians is a final fact. His interpretation of federalism is basically American. It could not encompass those who were concerned with being a nation, only those who wanted to preserve charming residual customs.[9]

For Grant, Hurtig's interpretation of federalism — the interpretation of federalism that animates the opponents of Meech Lake — is, evidently, basically American.

So, when coming to grips with the legacy of *Lament*, its relation to contemporary socialism (and, more broadly, with Grant's) and further, with Grant's and the book's imputed or implicit stance on the FTA one must bear in mind Forbes' reminder that we are dealing with a complex book. In the first place, it is Grant's relationship to socialism that is most at issue between Horowitz and Warren. In his talk, Warren conceded that there was some truth to Horowitz's well-known view that there is an affinity between Toryism (hence between Grant) and socialism: both doctrines sense that "social order is prior to liberty." But while toryism and socialism have "order" in common, they emphatically do not have "collectivism" in common ; Horowitz's observation that "toryism is a variant of collectivism" is, Warren asserts, "absurd."

In his contribution to this volume, Horowitz shifts ground slightly, and adds "egalitarianism" to "order" and "collectivism" in the discussion of the possible ideological links between Grant and socialism. Horowitz quotes an explicitly egalitarian passage from an older Grant essay, "An Ethic for Community." Warren, however, had earlier questioned the connection not between Grant and egalitarianism, but between socialism and egalitarianism: Horowitz himself appealed to Grant, Warren said, because "here was a leftist who actually was animated by a kind of egalitarian spirit. This is very rare, left or right." So: Horowitz believes that toryism — to which Grant undeniably subscribed — and socialism, are two versions of collectivism, and that George Grant and socialists alike are egalitarians. Warren, by contrast, believes that tories are not collectivists and that socialists are not egalitarians, and so tries to break Horowitz's double connection between Grant and socialism. There the argument stands.

There are of course, things to be said on both sides, but one cannot easily find them in *Lament*. "Collectivism" and "egalitarianism" figure neither in the language nor among the central concerns of the book. Before looking at what Grant does have to say in *Lament*'s most central discussion of socialism, it is important to note that there is one sense in which the book not only displays socialist (or, as Grant often put it, "Marxist") political sympathies, but employs socialist — and, in fact, Marxist — methodological assumptions: as Kim Campbell noted, the book "appears to rely upon an economic determinism that would make the crustiest Marxist smile." Beyond the questions of Grant's views on "order," "collectivism" and "egalitarianism," and the diverse connections each of these concepts may have with socialism, there is the indisputable matter of determinism in *Lament*, and of the exclusive engagement of determinism with Marxism: Marxist notions of legitimation and reductionism weave themselves through the book.

More centrally, though, whatever Grant's particular affinity for socialism in *Lament*, it can be understood only in the context of his depiction of conservatism and liberalism. Consider conservatism first. Conservatives of the American variety, Grant writes, are "old-fashioned liberals," for what they conserve "is the liberal philosophy of Locke," not the "organic conservatism" of Hooker[10]. Because the conservatism of Hooker "pre-date[d] the age of progress,"[11] it pre-dated the founding of the Republic and thus failed — as the subsequent wave of Lockean liberalism did not — to become part of the founding which American conservatives would conserve. And if American conservatives conserve a prior Lockian liberalism, conservatives more generally, including Canadian conservatives, conserve a somewhat more generic, ongoing progressivism. Such conservatives "can be no more than the defenders of whatever structure of power is at any moment necessary to technological change."[12]

If conservatism is a synonym for the values of liberalism, then liberalism is but a stalking horse for tyranny: liberalism makes the "universal and homogeneous state ... the pinnacle of political striving. 'Universal' implies a world-wide state,... 'homogeneous' means that all men would be equal," and therefore, all local cultures become "anachronistic."[13] According to the ancients, and hence according to Grant himself, "a universal and homogeneous state would be tyranny."[14] And the reason why liberalism consigns all particularities to the dust-heap is simply because, as Janet Azjenstadt suggests, it has not stopped at preserving individual rights, but has gone on to erode collective rights, which it regards as "anachronistic." Grant illustrates this characteristic of liberalism in his discussion of Diefenbaker's stance towards Quebec: "Insofar as he did not distinguish between the rights of individuals and the rights of nations, [insofar as he embraced pluralism for individuals but not for national communities] Diefenbaker showed himself to be a liberal"[15] On the one hand, then, conservatism — in "post-dating" the organic — doesn't go back far enough; it has, as David Warren points out, lost its memory. Instead, it can argue only for a "return to the individualism of the founding fathers";[16] its exemplars are Barry Goldwater and Milton Friedman. And on the other hand, liberalism, in rendering "anachronistic" all particularities and relegating them to the category of "charming residual customs,"[17] has gone too far; it has abandoned the rights of communities in favour of the overweening imperative of the rights of individuals.

What of socialism and Marxism? On the one hand, Grant writes, Marxism thinks of itself as an ideology of progress and human emancipation, and so seems to be a theory of complete individual freedom and mastery. But on the other hand, it contains a particular doctrine of teleology and a particular understanding of human alienation and so implicitly contains a theory of social order and the good, as well as an idea of the limits that can be placed on freedom in their name. "The vaunted freedom of the individual"[18] includes the freedom to fulfill the passion of greed.

> Yet what is socialism, if it is not the use of the government to restrain greed in the name of social good? In actual practice, socialism has always had to advocate inhibition in this respect. In doing so, was it not appealing to the conservative idea of social order against the liberal idea of freedom?[19]

Thus, unlike conservatism (an ideology whose memory reaches back to the individualism of Locke but stops short of the communitarianism of Hooker) and liberalism (an ideology of individual rights which has gone too far and revoked those rights from communities), socialism is capable of putting the brakes on individualism in the name of order and the good. But it is important to note that socialism can make this claim only by virtue of timing: for while "in the short run they have always been advocates of greater control over freedom," socialists "maintain that their policies would lead in the long run to a society of unrestricted freedom."[20] But as Grant points out, "Marx is not purely a philosopher of the age of progress; he is rooted in the teleological philosophy that pre-dates the age of progress."[21] The language of timing — pre-dates, short run, long run — is revealing: where conservatism is no longer the organic conservatism that "pre-dated the age of progress," socialism is rooted in a teleological philosophy that does pre-date the age of progress. And where liberalism has made order and community "anachronistic," we are still living in the "shortrun" of socialism, in which order and the good can still serve to counterbalance the imperatives of freedom and mastery. The superiority of socialism over conservatism and liberalism is contingent, depending as it does on the timing of its advent and the pace of its development.

Grant, though, offers no reason to believe that socialism might not eventually lose its memory of teleology just as conservatism lost its memory of organicism; nor does he provide any assurance that, as the short run becomes the long run, socialists will not jettison the primacy of social order for the prerogatives of individual freedom. Indeed, in "In Defense of North America," published four years after *Lament*, Grant says that it is the conservatives — "the 'right'" — who now "want it both ways," who "want to maintain certain moral customs ... which are not in fact compatible with advancing technological civilization," and who therefore advance a "mixture of individualism and public order."[22] And it is "those of the 'left'" — "domestic Marxists" — who "appeal exclusively to the redemptive possibilities of technology," and who "concentrate on the libertarian and Utopian expectations in their doctrines because unlike the Marxists of the East they could leave the requirements of public order to others."[23] Four years after *Lament*, it is the conservatives who would restrain individualism with order, and the Marxists who have abandoned teleology for technology. *Lament*'s philosophical preference such as it is for socialism is fundamentally contingent.

If, on the matter of socialism, Grant's legacy as the author of *Lament* is contingent, then on the question of the FTA, it is ambivalent. In considering *Lament* in the context of the 1988 election, what emerges most strongly from the book is the antinomy between two concepts which Grant continually evokes — "parochialism" and "progress." Interestingly, these two words, during the 1988 campaign, were at the very heart of Brian Mulroney's boilerplate hustings speech — though, of course, boilerplate Brian Mulroney is a proponent of "progress" and an opponent of "parochialism," and the Grant of *Lament* is quite straightforwardly a critic of "progress" and a defender, or at least a mourner, of "parochialism." It is noteworthy that in the central argument of *Lament*, Grant wasn't afraid to use language that stacked the deck against him; he acknowledged the virtues of progress and the privations of parochialism, and yet he still made a compelling case against the former, in favour of the latter.

There is no need to draw any blasphemous parallels here between Grant and Mulroney as political thinkers or even as individuals. But certainly boilerplate Mulroney and the author of *Lament* each at some level, see Canada as being faced with an enduring polarity or choice. The critics of the Free Trade Agreement, in contrast, did not speak at all in that idiom, and so to that extent cannot claim to be Grant's legatees. For one thing, in response to Mulroney's jibes, instead of defending parochialism as Grant did, they avowed that they were not, in fact, parochialists, but rather, that they were internationalists. In contrast to the continentalism they saw embodied in the FTA, they proposed the multilateralism of the General Agreement on Tariffs and Trade. And in response to Mulroney's taunt that they were "Luddites," the FTA critics did not, as the author of *Lament* would have done, cogently respond with an attack on progress: they claimed that they were not opposed to progress. They were only against the unbridled, "free-enterprise" brand of progress which they associated with the FTA, preferring instead a more statist, managed version. The opponents of the FTA thus wanted to efface, to evade, the hard choice posed by both Grant and Mulroney, by arguing that the evils of parochialism could be dissolved, while its benefits preserved, through an active internationalism, and that the evils of progress could be tempered and its benefits gleaned, through a philosophy of state management of the socioeconomy.

Grant himself, however, was not so disingenuous. In *Lament*, he claimed that internationalism is just as inconsistent with "sovereignty" and "parochialism" as continentalism is. In fact, internationalism is merely a stalking horse for continentalism — in the Canadian setting, internationalism means continentalism — just as those who advocate continentalism do so because they honestly see it as a move towards, not away from, internationalism: they believe that continentalism must be a step towards a nobler internationalism. And if Mel Hurtig's internationalism and Simon Riesman's continentalism are moral — or amoral — equivalents in Grant's eyes, so too are the twin versions of progress, the state-managed and the laissez-faire varieties. In the 1988 election, on a political level, the author of *Lament* would have found the internationalist-statist-progressivism of Broadbent-Turner as problematic as the continentalist-free-enterprise-progressivism of Mulroney. And on an idiomatic level, Grant would have found Mulroney — and not Broadbent-Turner — speaking his language.

NOTES

1   George Grant, *Lament for a Nation — The Defeat of Canadian Nationalism.* (Ottawa: Carleton University Press, 1989), p. 64.

2   Ibid., p. 15.

3   Ibid., p. 17.

4   Ibid., p. 44.

5   Ibid., p. 39.

6   Ibid., p. 40.

7   Ibid., p. 5.

8   Ibid., p. 96.

9   Ibid., p. 21.

10   Ibid., p. 65.

11   Ibid., p. 56.

12   Ibid., p. 67.

13   Ibid., p. 53, 54.

14   Ibid., p. 96.

15   Ibid., p. 22.

16   Ibid., p. 65.

17   Ibid., p. 21.

18   Ibid., p. 57.

19   Ibid., p. 59.

20   Ibid.

21   Ibid., p. 56.

22   Grant, "In Defence of North America", *Technology and Empire — Perspectives on North America*. (Toronto: House of Anansi Press Limited, 1969), p. 30.

23   Ibid., pp. 30-31.

PART III

THE REVIVAL OF POLITICAL PHILOSOPHY

GEORGE GRANT
AND THE REVIVAL OF
POLITICAL PHILOSOPHY

Barry Cooper

To say that the term "political philosophy" had been popularized by Leo Strauss would be to exaggerate greatly. To imagine that the
practice of political philosophy could be popularized at all is evidence
of a want of understanding. One may say, however, that Leo Strauss
gave the term a precision that it had previously lacked. I have been
asked to speak on the topic of George Grant and the revival of political
philosophy. I would like to begin by recalling Strauss' words.

Political philosophy means two different but related things.
From the first point of view, it is a branch of philosophy:

> ...'philosophy' indicates the manner of treatment: a
> treatment which both goes to the roots and is compre-
> hensive; 'political' indicates both the subject matter
> and the function: political philosophy deals with politi-
> cal matters in a way that is meant to be relevant for
> political life.[1]

But if political philosophy is relevant for political life, it will be
addressed to citizens, not just to philosophers:

> From this [second] point of view the adjective 'politi-
> cal' in the expression 'political philosophy' designates
> not so much a subject matter as a manner of
> treatment,...not the philosophic treatment of politics,

but the political or popular treatment of philosophy, or the introduction to philosophy — the attempt to lead the qualified citizens, or rather their qualified sons, from the political life to the philosophical life.[2]

George Grant came to understand these words as applying to his own work.

In *Technology and Justice* (1986) Grant called himself "a political philosopher within Christianity."[3] Before the publication of that book, however, he used other terms to describe himself and his work. Moreover, one must consider the meaning of the qualifying phrase, "within Christianity." Grant characterized *Lament for a Nation*, the book that secured his reputation, particularly among Canadian intellectuals and opinion leaders as based "not on philosophy but on tradition."[4] *Technology and Empire*, he said, "did not presume to be philosophy, but [was] written out of the study of the history of political philosophy."[5] One may conclude, therefore, that prior to *Technology and Justice* Grant may not have considered himself a political philosopher. Let me suggest one reason for this. First, students of Grant's writings have detected three "phases" in his work.[6] Grant himself, however, has made the following observation:

> For whatever else may be said about the philosophers who related their doctrine on political matters to their desire to have knowledge of the whole, among the best of them there has been a monumental consistency which related their doctrine on one issue to what they taught on all others.[7]

Grant, in contrast, freely admitted to having changed his thought on certain fundamental questions.

Philosophers, according to Grant, are consistent in that their political teachings are intelligibly integrated with their larger doctrines and desires. Grant has placed his emphasis on the first meaning of Strauss' term. Let us conclude, perhaps too quickly, that by this understanding, Grant was not a philosopher. The next question is obvious: if not a philosopher, then what was he?

We may begin to answer the question by reflecting on a passage from a somewhat unlikely source — Nietzsche. In *Thus Spoke Zarathustra*, there is an amusing section titled "On Scholars" (II:16). We learn there that Zarathustra was himself once a scholar and he knew their ways, which were the ways of sheep: "As I lay asleep, a sheep ate of the ivy wreath on my brow—ate and said, 'Zarathustra is no longer a scholar.' Said it, and strutted away proudly. A child told it to me."[9] To children, as to thistles and poppies, Zarathustra was still a scholar. "They are innocent even in their malice. But to the sheep I am no longer a scholar: thus my lot decrees it. Bless it!"[10] The sheep/scholar was certain of his own superiority, which is why he strutted off proudly; still, he confined himself to nibbling leaves from Zarathustra's brow. At the very least, scholars are easily persuaded, perhaps as a matter of taste, of their superiority.

Zarathustra went on:

> For this is the truth: I have moved from the house of the scholars and I even banged the door behind me. My soul sat hungry at their table too long; I am not, like them, trained to pursue knowledge as if it were nutcracking.[10]

Scholars, Zarathustra indicated, are problem-solvers. He also characterized them as petty parasites: "...they wait and gape at thoughts that others have thought....They are skillful and have clever fingers.... All threading and knotting and weaving their fingers understand: thus they knit the socks of the spirit."[12] But scholars were also consistent, "good clockworks," so long as they were wound up correctly. "Then they indicate the hour without fail and make a modest noise."[13] But, he said, they watch each other "like spiders." They prepare poison for each other and play with loaded dice.

Zarathustra's relationship to the scholar/sheep was complex. That they no longer considered him a scholar was, no doubt, a blessing. Their house was stifling and, Zarathustra said, "I love freedom and the air over the fresh earth; rather would I sleep on ox hides than on their decorums and respectabilities."[14] Moreover, Zarathustra, unlike the respectable scholars, needed to go "into the open and away from all dusty rooms" in order to think; but "they sit cool in the cool shade: in everything, they want to be mere spectators, and they beware of sitting where the sun burns on the steps."[15] Outside in the hot sun, Zarathustra's thoughts nearly take his breath away; but the scholars, cool as cucumbers, gape. "We are alien to each other," said Zarathustra, and their virtues were even more obnoxious to him than their falseness and their cheating.

> And when I lived with them, I lived above them. That is why they developed a grudge against me. They did not want to hear how someone was living over their heads; and so they put wood and earth and filth between me and their heads. Thus they muffled the sound of my steps: and so far I have been heard least well by the most scholarly. Between themselves and me they laid all human faults and weaknesses: "false ceilings" they call them in their houses. And yet I live over their heads with my thoughts; and even if I wanted to walk upon my own mistakes, I would still be over their heads.[16]

George Grant and Nietzsche's Zarathustra would disagree about many things. Grant would not have concurred with Zarathustra's next words, for example: "For men are not equal: thus speaks justice. And what I want, they would have no right to want! Thus spoke Zarathustra."[17] Nor, among many other things, would he agree with Zarathustra's teaching on marriage (I:20). I mention this only in the hope of avoiding misunderstanding when I say that George Grant was not a scholar. Children of a certain kind still see him that way, however. Their malice is innocent insofar as they are ignorant and unaware of themselves. In either case they are a long way from political philosophy.

Others are likewise filled with malice, but are not so innocent. Like Zarathustra's scholar/sheep, intellectuals have nibbled at Grant's laurels. They have devoured the leaves that wreathed his brow and walked away, muttering to themselves even as they quoted. Whether or not they agreed with what George Grant had written, most were convinced of their superiority. Part of the legacy of *Lament for a Nation* must include this phenomenon.

More subtle indications of George Grant's relationship to the scholars appeared even before *Lament for a Nation* made his work useful to intellectuals. In 1958 he published an article on philosophy in the *Encyclopedia Canadiana*. Grant remarked that the University of

Toronto was "the centre of English philosophic teaching in Canada, particularly at the doctorate level,"[18] which sounds like praise. The emphasis in the University of Toronto Philosophy Department, he went on, has been on the scholarly activity of intellectual history. "All the varying traditions of classical and European philosophy are investigated, expounded and analyzed."[19] This activity has produced "able works," the purpose of which has been prophylactic:

> It has prevented Canadian philosophy from being dominated by the linguistic emphasis that characterizes contemporary English and American thought. Its main danger of inadequacy, perhaps, is that academic philosophers may be led to confine themselves to history and to living in silence before the urgent present of society.[20]

Grant went on to praise the scholastic philosophers of the great Quebec universities for having played such a formative role in that community: "...there the contemplative life has been encouraged as necessary for the community and noble in itself."[21] No one in the Philosophy Department at the University of Toronto, or in any philosophy department elsewhere in Canada looking to the University of Toronto as to the city on a hill, could but take umbrage at such remarks.

A few years earlier, in his study for the Massey Commission, Grant had made much the same point. "The study of philosophy," he said, "is the analysis of the traditions of our society and the judgement of those traditions against our varying intuitions of the Perfection of God."[22] So understood, philosophy is the rational, as distinct from the mystical or aesthetic, form of the account of our own activity and of the activity of others. It is not, therefore, "confined to a subject found in university calendars," although universities are privileged sites for the practice of philosophy. Grant went on to say that it was a "truism" that Canadian universities did not encourage the young "to think about their world in the broadest and deepest way."[23] Again, one could hear the hackles rise in philosophy departments across the land. Grant's closing words were even more of an offence.

> The present writer has no alternative but to repeat once again his conviction that the practice of philosophy (and for that matter, all the arts of civilization) will

depend on a prior condition — namely the intensity
and concentration of our faith in God."[24]

In a conversation with William Christian,[25] Grant indicated that the scholars were indeed offended. They had knit their socks of the spirit and had prepared their poisons. For his part, George Grant had moved from the house of the scholars and had banged the door behind him.

Very well: not wishing to be thought children, we allow that Grant was not a Zarathustran scholar. But we have no wish to be thought of as scholar/sheep, strutting proudly away after pronouncing: "Zarathustra and Grant are no longer scholars." By Grant's own reckoning he was a traditionalist at the time of *Lament for a Nation* (1965) and a student of the history of political philosophy at the time of *Technology and Empire* (1969), but these are not very precise terms. Their imprecision and Grant's acknowledged inconsistencies may provide us with a clue as to what Grant actually was.

Within the ambit of Nietzsche's vocabulary one might say that Grant was a "philosophical labourer." George Grant might not be entirely pleased with this, for the following reason. Philosophical labourers, Nietzsche said, were dependent upon those "genuine philosophers" who are "commanders and legislators," whose knowing is creating, and whose will to truth is will to power.[26] We may judge this a fatal objection. Even so, one must allow that Grant would be in good company. The "noble models" are Kant and Hegel, whose "enormous and wonderful task" had been to make everything that has happened and been esteemed "easy to look over, easy to think over, intelligible and manageable."[27] This purpose is surely akin to Strauss' second sense of political philosophy. Moreover, Grant has surely undertaken that enormous and wonderful task for us, and we should be grateful for what we have learned.

These reflections indicate that Grant was not a philosopher in the sense that he understood the term, nor a scholar in Nietzsche's sense. Like Nietzsche's Zarathustra, he slammed the door on the house of scholars, but he did so in the name of an understanding of philosophy that would not have been shared by Nietzsche. Even so, both Grant and Zarathustra considered scholars to be living metaphorically under the false ceilings of their own construction. Even if they walked upon their mistakes, they would be over the heads of the cool scholar spectators.

Let me be more explicit: George Grant was a thinker, not a scholar or a philosopher. This remark is more explicit, of course, only if one already knows what thinking is. Fortunately, you in this audience, like all other sane humans and probably many humans who are called crazy, do know what thinking is. Let me remind you, then, of what you all already know. In the *Meno* (80e) we learn from Socrates that "a man cannot try to discover either what he knows or what he does not know. If he knows, there is no need of inquiry; if he does not know...he does not even know what he is to look for."[28] Or, in the *Euthyphro* we learn that, in order to be pious, we must know what piety is. The things that please the gods are pious things. But are they pious because they please the gods? Or do they please the gods because they are pious? One of my better students once told me that considering such questions made her head hurt. That, it seems to me, is precisely the point of thinking: to induce perplexity. Socrates was not a clever professor. In the *Charmides* (165b-c) he told Critias that he had nothing to teach: "Critias, you act as if I professed to know the answers to the questions I ask you and could give you answers if I wished. It is not so, I enquire with you...because I lack knowledge myself."[29]

Socrates was investigating, with Critias and Meno and the others, the meanings of words such as piety and beauty. In the more differentiated vocabulary of mediaeval philosophy, this mental activity was called meditation. Now, meditation or thinking as an activity was, like all activities, undertaken for a purpose. In Grant's essay in the Massey Commission Report, he said thinking aimed at measuring our traditions against our varying intuitions of the perfection of God. This was a highly mediaeval sentiment and understanding. At the end of his essay he quoted A.N. Whitehead to buttress his opinion: "...in the ages of faith men pursued truth and beauty," said Whitehead, "whereas sceptics fail for want of faith and abandon the 'tiring discipline of being rational.'"[30] As I understand it, Grant was indicating that the purpose of thought was to open the eyes of the mind, to use an Aristotelean formula. Or, in the Christian terminology he preferred, the purpose of meditation was to prepare the soul for intuitions of the perfection of God.

To summarize this account of Grant's activity: it consisted in thinking or in meditative exegesis. But what did Grant think about? Or, what was the meditative exegesis he undertook? In his *Encyclopedia Canadiana* article, Grant indicated that philosophical scholarship or academic philosophy was in danger of "living in silence before the urgent present of society." The revival of political philosophy is, I believe, directly connected to the urgent present.

We see the connection clearly in the collected works of three people, namely, Eric Voegelin, Leo Strauss and Hannah Arendt. All three were directly touched by the urgent present. Arendt's *Origins of Totalitarianism* has lost none of its importance in the era of global technology. Voegelin opened his *New Science of Politics* with the observation that, "when the order of a society flounders and disintegrates, the fundamental problems of political existence in history are more apt to come into view than in periods of comparative stability."[31] I believe that insight is borne out by the example of George Grant's reflections on justice, which is surely *the* question for political philosophy, in the modern technological-liberal world. Indeed, as Grant himself remarked on the opening page of *English-Speaking Justice*: "The first task of thought in our era is to think what that technology is: to think it in its determining power over our politics and sexuality, our music and education."[32] The importance of Strauss, however, was of a different order.

It would not be much of an exaggeration to say that Leo Strauss was one of the most provocative thinkers ever to disturb the minds, if not the souls, of academic political scientists. In his introduction to a recent collection of Strauss' writings, Professor Tom Pangle spent several pages describing the accusatory reception of Strauss' work. Strauss' pupils have had their own disputes with one another, as may be expected, and as many of you know. What is worthier of mention, however, is that Strauss has had respectable interlocutors as well as carping critics: among others, Alexandre Kojeve, Eric Voegelin, C.B. Macpherson, Raymond Aron, Karl Loewith, Emil Fackenheim, Hans-Georg Gadamer, and Arnaldo Momigliano. These men, one may say, were Strauss' peers. When George Grant refers to Strauss, one has the feeling that in Strauss' work Grant found what he was looking for, at least as far as political philosophy was concerned.

Towards the end of his Introduction to the second edition of *Philosophy in the Mass Age*, Grant explains how he came to understand the importance of political philosophy through Strauss' work. For the next few minutes I would like to consider this text. To understand the significance of Grant's remarks about Strauss, it is necessary to mention another thinker who influenced him, Jacques Ellul. Ellul was not a political philosopher and his books are not usually called political philosophy. They are, perhaps, sociology. Of Ellul's major work, *The Technological Society*, Grant said, "The structure of modern society is made plain as in nothing else I have read."[33] And in modern technological society Grant found the chief impediment to achieving clarity about "moral philosophy." By moral philosophy Grant meant the science that "attempts to answer the question, 'What constitutes the good life?'" [34]

Under the best of circumstances, moral philosophy "is therefore a science in which it is difficult to achieve clarity."[35] Ellul's description of the technological society or of "the dominance of technique over all aspects of our lives"[36] was, accordingly, an account of what made clarity about moral philosophy more difficult than it needs be. As many of you know already, Grant's remarks on technology constitute much of his refusal to live "in silence before the urgent present of society," which, you will recall, is the besetting temptation or weakness of academic philosophy as practised by scholars.

The dominance of technique or the triumph of the technological society has meant, in everyday terms, the widespread belief that all human problems can be solved and the means to do it is a kind of technical skill. To the extent that morality consists of conventions and insights as to the right way of doing things, "today it can be truly said that the only living morality of our society is faith in technique."[37] We forget about this, Grant said, because we are convinced that technology can be used for good or for evil, according to the will or the "values" of the user. This cliche assumes that technology is the servant not the master of humans. Ellul had convinced Grant that the opposite was true, that "the dominance of technique over all aspects of our lives" was the pervasive everyday reality. Two implications followed for moral philosophy: first, the pursuit of technological change or, as one conventionally says, the pursuit of progress, is taken to constitute human excellence and hence morality. Second, in order for this account of morality to have triumphed, other accounts (identified by Grant as those moral traditions of the past which doubted the dogma that human beings could solve all their problems by technique) had to be ridiculed. One must point out that these other moral traditions were neither criticized nor found in some way defective. They were ridiculed.

The results of this voluntary and deliberate deculturation are perplexing. In Grant's words, one finds oneself "in a new relation to tradition."[38] Now, tradition sanctifies the past, preserves it by handing over or handing down from one generation to the next, the teachings of the ancestors, which in turn were authoritative. The "new relation" of which Grant wrote is this: instead of sanctifying the past our modern tradition repudiates it or desanctifies it. But if the past is not worth preserving, what is to be handed over? The future, perhaps? Grant's perplexity was expressed in a paradoxical observation: "We live in a society where more men worship the same god than ever before, but the cult of that god can find no easily fixed forms."[39] But in the absence of fixed forms, how can one worship at all? Further paradoxes followed. The "theology of technique," Grant said, "goes by the name of liberalism," which is "the belief that man's essence is his freedom."[40]

To be more precise and less paradoxical, liberalism is the civil theology of the technological society and far more effective in this respect than Marxism. Now most individuals, Grant said, have no need for the difficult science of moral philosophy. What they do need is a civil theology, "liberal sermons." If they become more sophisticated, he went on, they need "the systematic exposition of progressive dogma."[41] There are plenty of sermonizers and dogmatics around "for it is always easy to find flatterers of the spirit of the age."[42] In his subsequent writings Grant elaborated on many of these themes, but by then he had adopted as his own many of the insights of political philosophy. In this 1966 Introduction he was caught, so to speak, in the midst of a discovery.

To recapitulate: liberalism is the civil theology of the technological society and the dogma of progress is its systematic exposition. In popular or refined form, these teachings have eclipsed moral philosophy. To provide an analysis of such things is possible only if one is not a simple believer in them. Grant, therefore, had somehow resisted the deculturation sufficiently to be able to analyze it. His account of how this was possible was almost passive in its simplicity. "Men being what they are,"[43] he said, some are dissatisfied with the moral philosophy contained in the worship of technology and expressed in liberalism. "Men being what they are" explains, apparently, the existence of people who "still [hunger] for the bread of eternal life in the midst of the modern dynamism"; when this occurs, one "must seek to satisfy that hunger."[44]

It seems true enough that one must seek to satisfy such a hunger. What I wish to emphasize here is that what gives rise to the hunger remains at least in part a mystery. I have no objection to terms such as miracle, providence, or grace. But I would say that they express the same mystery; they do not dispel it.

Somehow, then, this experience of dissatisfaction with the reigning civil theology arises. Then what? "As the past has been demolished as a living continuity," Grant said, "men can no longer inherit it in their day-to-day lives; they must set themselves the task of being miners of the buried past." To undertake the task of mining the past, Grant assured us, is a serious not merely a scholarly business. It is not antiquarian; it is, rather, "a search for good which can be appropriated to the present." The first step is to consider or "chart" the moral philosophy of the present. The difficulty of so doing makes moral philosophy "such a perilous task in our age."[45]

Granted that moral philosophy is difficult, it is not self-evident that it is also perilous. A perilous task is one that is full of risks. One wonders what could be risky about moral philosophy. Supposing one failed to chart the course of modern moral philosophy, one could still write a book about it. *Philosophy in the Mass Age*, Grant said, was a kind of failure. But surely it was not such a failure that he was fired from McMaster for having written it. Indeed, precisely because of the difficulties inherent in moral philosophy, even a bad book, and one that is not even about moral philosophy, will help you get tenure. Many of us know this from personal experience and from sitting on tenure and promotion committees.

Grant's meaning lay elsewhere. Let me indicate what he meant with an analogy. Just outside Banff townsite stands Mt. Rundle. Some of you know all too well that attaining the summit of Mt. Rundle can be a perilous task. Failure to exercise one's skill at scrambling can result in more than just a bad day's climb. Here a difficult task is also risky and perilous. The difficulty of the climb measures one's skills in charting a course to the top, and failure puts one's being in peril. Grant was suggesting that charting the course of modern philosophy risked his being, and not merely his scholarly skills or talents. This could hardly be otherwise if one understood philosophy as Grant did, as "the analysis of the traditions of our society and the judgement of those traditions against our varying intuitions of the Perfection of God." This is also what made the next few paragraphs of his Introduction autobiographical.

Philosophy in the Mass Age, he said, was written when his mind was "deeply divided" about the relationship between moral tradition and progress. He had received, by chance, "some glimmering" of what belief in an eternal order meant, so that he "was no longer totally held by the liberal faith." He had certain practical reservations about technology but, "I was still held by the progressive dogma." Grant explained his thraldom with reference to life in North America: faith in progress "is the very ground of their [North Americans'] being." To call into question the benefits of technology in North America, to cast doubt on "the trust in that science which issues in the conquest of nature, human and non-human," he said, is to appear as a "neurotic seeking to escape from life into dreams."[46] To use his earlier language, if moral philosophy is concerned with what constitutes the good life or with the nature of human excellence, then any attempt, within the technological milieu, to relate human excellence to that milieu will appear neurotic. Put positively: for those who have benefited from technology, which means nearly everyone in North America, the technological society embodied the good life and constituted the highest incarnation of human excellence. That is what Grant meant by saying that faith in progress was the very ground of being for North Americans. The perilousness of moral philosophy consisted in calling into question the ground of being of modern North American life. If not progress, then what?

Philosophy in the Mass Age, Grant continued, could not raise that question, let alone answer it. It was true enough that much had been lost to technology, but Grant "balanced" that fact against the belief that all would soon be regained "and regained at a higher level because of the leisure made possible by technology."[47] Grant believed in technology with a human face, in the possibility that "our society would have within itself all that was good in the antique world and yet keep all the benefits of technology."[48] Comparing this with Grant's other remarks concerning technology leaves one with a sense of wonder at the depth of his conversion. I would like, therefore, to make plain what exactly was "deeply divided" about George Grant's views when he wrote *Philosophy in the Mass Age*.

The evidence was clear enough and it was acknowledged by Grant's common sense. First, "we were losing the idea that morality had any eternal reference, that we were entering a society where anything goes"; second, "contemplation of final cause was disappearing from the multiversities which served our system"; third, "art had lost all reference beyond the subjective and entertaining."[49] These were, to state the matter boldly, facts. And yet they were transfigured by belief into a "stage" that was shortly to be transcended. How was the magic to be accomplished? How was Grant convinced that the darkness was the darkness before dawn?

The answer, in a word, was Hegel. In Grant's view, Hegel was "the greatest of all philosophers" not least of all because he had synthesized "all that was true and beautiful in the Greek world" with Christianity and with "the freedom of the enlightenment and modern science." Moreover, Grant said, it was difficult in the extreme to "believe in the western Christian doctrine of providence" and not also to conclude with Hegel on virtually everything else.[50] *Philosophy in the Mass Age*, therefore, was a kind of Hegelian *livre de circonstance* in which Grant "attempted to write down in non-professional language the substance of the vision that the age of reason was beginning to dawn and first in North America."[51] Anyone who has read Hegel with care, Stanley Rosen once said, is bound to take practical matters very seriously indeed. Grant had obviously done just that.

But, he went on, "Since that day my mind has changed."[52] Grant did not say, "I changed my mind," as if it were an act of volition. Nor did he say, "my mind was changed," as if he were the patient of some therapy. The locution indicates persuasion. Grant did not immediately indicate the source of his persuasion, but turned instead to an account of changes in his judgements. In "the practical realm" the consequences for the individuals who make up the technological society were not good. Technology was not a means to be used for better or for worse. It was a kind of end, the pursuit of which inhibited "the pursuit of other ends in the society it controls." Accordingly, the chief consequence of a technological society is that it debases "our conceptions of human excellence." When one loses sight of genuine excellence, it is not easily recovered. On the other hand, when one realizes that the technological society has debased human excellence, it is a "terrible moment."[53] One might describe this terrible moment as one of deep dissatisfaction with what exists coupled with a pervasive awareness of one's uncertainty about what has been lost. Grant's experience is, I believe, widely shared today. We may have, for example, grave doubts about existing industrial policies, and yet we are not reassured by anti-industrial zealots.

Grant concluded his reflections on the "practical realm" with the following remark: "...unlimited technological development presents an undoubted threat to the possibility of human excellence." Having learned as much, "One can thereafter only approach modern society with fear and perhaps trembling and, above all, with caution."[54] Grant's prudent reminder of the need for caution is worth recollecting when we witness today opponents of technology possessed with the same inner self-certainty that Grant found a generation ago on the side of the proponents of the technological society.

Related to his changed assessment of the practical realm was his "reassessment of the truth of modern political philosophy."[55] One can quickly think of sound Hegelian grounds for moving from the practical to the reflective. When *Philosophy in the Mass Age* was written Grant believed that Hegel was the greatest of philosophers and that the age of reason was about to dawn in North America. Indeed, Hegel's account of the Western Christian doctrine of providence was decisive in sustaining Grant's belief about the new era of reason and about its location. But having come to understand what was happening in North America as a threat to the possibility of human excellence rather than as its fulfillment, Grant was led to reassess the account of things that sustained his earlier and now rejected opinion. But Hegel is not so easy to reject. No great philosopher is.

One must, of course, speak in a kind of code about these matters, since it is possible to study Hegel for a lifetime and never glimpse what Northrop Frye might call the circumference of his thought. Grant was aware of the compression and brevity of his account. He said he had to reassess the truth of modern philosophy in light of the significance of technology. One is reminded of another reassessment, by Emil Fackenheim, of Hegel's philosophy in light of the Nazi extermination policies.[56] By "modern philosophy" Grant meant more than just Hegel, though Hegel remained a significant figure in the picture-gallery of the modern spirit. Modern philosophy included "the thought which has emerged in western European civilization in the last four or five centuries" and that was, in Grant's view, "more than any other source, responsible for the world we now inhabit." Accordingly, if one is led to question the goodness of modern society, one is also led to question "the ultimate presuppositions upon which its immediacies depend."[57] Those presuppositions are found in modern philosophy.

One cannot simply question modern philosophy because it seems to be connected to a social order one rejects. Such *ab extra* "critical thought" has become a kind of professional deformation of intellectuals and "social critics," but it is by no means a philosophical act or even a serious enterprise. If we are to question the ultimate presuppositions of modern philosophy, "we are driven to look elsewhere for more adequate accounts," and the "obvious place for a western man to look is to the Greek philosophers."[58] Now, Hegel has looked to the Greek philosophers too, so it was necessary to look to the Greek philosophers in a non-Hegelian way. Grant did so, apparently. At any rate, he came to the conclusion, after studying Plato and Aristotle, "that Hegel was not correct in his claim to have taken the truth of antique thought and synthesized it with the modern to produce a higher (and perhaps highest) truth." In particular, Grant was persuaded that "Plato's account of what constitutes human excellence and the possibility of its realization in the world is more valid than that of Hegel."[59] Grant's "brief description" of his change of mind was terse indeed. Its significance, however, was plain.

The Introduction to *Philosophy in the Mass Age* is George Grant's acknowledgement of his debt to classical political philosophy. He explained clearly that he found in Plato's teaching on human excel-

lence a means to resist the grip of the progressive dogma. The seriousness of his reflection is measured by the difficulty one has in overcoming one's faith in progress. This understanding of Grant's relation to
the revival of political philosophy is confirmed by his many remarks.
We have already mentioned Ellul. Grant went on to say that, "Concerning the more difficult and more important theoretical questions,
my debt is above all to the writings of Leo Strauss." His concluding
sentence was as follows: "As the greatest joy and that most difficult of
attainment is any movement of the mind (however small) towards
enlightenment, I count it a high blessing to have been acquainted with
this man's thought."[60]

Grant's Introduction was dated 1966. Three years earlier he
had published an article in *Social Research*, "Tyranny and Wisdom: The
Controversy Between L. Strauss and A. Kojeve," which dealt in some
detail with one of the more difficult and more important theoretical
questions.[61] In that article Grant presented a synopsis of the dispute
between Kojeve and Strauss and then added two comments. By
Grant's account, Strauss and Kojeve discussed "whether the universal
and homogeneous state is the best social order." This way of posing the
topic was non-Hegelian in the extreme, which is to say that Grant
undertook a Straussian, not a Kojevian reading of the controversy. This
is not to say that Grant was a "Straussian," which is a recondite term
in any event. It is enough to say that Grant's relationship to the revival
of political philosophy was mediated by Strauss' understanding of
that revival.

Let me conclude by making two additional remarks. The first
is to outline what Strauss's understanding of the revival of political
philosophy entailed. The second is to suggest what Grant may have
perceived to be a limitation of that revival.

I mentioned earlier that Strauss' work has been controversial.
There are even controversies over why his work is controversial. I shall
try to ignore much of this interesting dispute and state, quite simply,
that I believe Tom Pangle chose well in calling his introductory
collection of the thought of Leo Strauss, *The Rebirth of Classical Political
Rationalism*. Classical political rationalism entailed several sentiments,
attitudes and arguments that one finds in Grant's thinking as well.

The first and most obvious thing to mention is that Grant followed Strauss in turning to the thinkers of the past for insight into the meaning of the present. Strauss wrote:

> "It is not self-forgetting and pain-loving antiquarianism nor self-forgetting and intoxicating romanticism which induces us to turn with passionate interest, with unqualified willingness to learn, toward the political thought of classical antiquity. We are impelled to do so by the crisis of our time, the crisis of the West."[62]

The parallel is not exact, but one might say that the "urgent present" for Strauss was expressed in the symbol "crisis of the West," whereas Grant preferred to speak of the incarnation of that crisis, the technological society.

Second, Grant followed Strauss' understanding of classical political philosophy in formulating many of his critical analyses of modern society. Grant, like Strauss, refused to flatter what he considered unworthy of praise. According to Grant, both liberal sermonizing and exposition of progressive dogma were common modes of intellectual discourse, used everywhere by the "flatterers of the spirit of the age." Strauss put it this way: "...we are not permitted to be flatterers of democracy precisely because we are friends and allies of democracy."[63] Third, where Grant spoke of the difficulties and perilousness of moral philosophy, Strauss used equivalent language to discuss virtue. Fourth, the refusal to flatter and the concern for virtue raises the question of a real or potential conflict between the thinker and his fellows.

In an early book, *Spinoza's Critique of Religion*, Strauss recalled the importance of Spinoza's concern with the "theological-political problem." Earlier in this paper the problem was introduced using Augustine's category, "civil theology." Much of the controversy surrounding Strauss concerns one of the ways in which philosophers have fixed the limits to civil theology. Strauss can hardly be said to have discovered the importance of rhetoric and what is usually called esoteric writing. Prior to the easy-going and superficial tolerance of liberalism, philosophers knew about the need for speech *ad capitum vulgi*. Strauss may be said to have assisted greatly in the rediscovery or recovery of several forgotten kinds of writing. Grant experienced first hand the reality which Strauss wrote about so beautifully, and he did so before reading Strauss' work.

In a conversation with William Christian, when asked why he had not written very much about religion, Grant said:

> I have written indirectly all my life for one reason and one reason alone: I think there has been — I don't think, I'm sure — in the last four centuries in the West, an intense and sustained attack on Christianity from within, and particularly by intellectual people.... There has been a sustained attack on Christianity. Therefore I would see my work as a defence of two figures, Socrates and Christ. For different reasons. And therefore I have always written indirectly because I knew that the intellectual world or the world I inhabited was very hostile to both the figures I chiefly admired. That's why I haven't written directly.[64]

Grant then mentioned, in characteristically demotic language, the unfriendly reception of his study on philosophy, written for the Massey Commission. It had taught him an obvious lesson:

> If I wanted to have anything to say in [Canadian universities], I had to speak very indirectly. It was probably all right to talk about Socrates. But it was not all right to talk about Christ. I think the main thing is that there has been a sustained hostility to Christianity, which was powerful but hidden.[65]

Grant's remarks are important in two respects. First, he was experientially prepared, *avant la lettre*, to receive one of Strauss' important teachings on the topic of rhetoric. Second, and perhaps more importantly, he sought to defend both Socrates *and* Christ. This remark by Grant returns us to the question of what it means to be "a political philosopher within Christianity."

The sense of the grammar indicates that political philosophy can be understood as existing within Christianity. It is unclear from Grant's remark about Socrates and Christ whether he meant that political philosophy was simply within Christianity or whether it was within Christianity *for him,* and therefore that Christianity might be within political philosophy for someone else. Clearly, political philosophy was within Christianity for Grant, and therefore the recovery of political philosophy, for all the blessings that followed, was not a soteriological event. It was an intellectual achievement of the highest order, but it was not marked by an eschatological index.

I point to two pieces of evidence. First, in his discussion of the Kojeve-Strauss dispute, Grant said of Strauss that his "reticence about Biblical religion puts him at a disadvantage" because, while he could criticize Kojeve's account of the place of Biblical religion in western history, "he is not able to state, except by implication, his own account of that history." And, Grant added, in his final words, "how can he maintain his reticence at this point."[66] The second piece of evidence is taken from "Faith and the Multiversity," in which Grant made a brief comparison of the death of Socrates and the death of Christ.

> Just before drinking the hemlock, Socrates makes a wonderful joke; in Gethsemane Christ's 'sweat was, as it were, great drops of blood falling to the ground.' Indeed, the difference is also stated in the fact that where Socrates' wife is absent for most of Phaedo, the two Marys stand beneath the cross.[67]

As for what this may mean, I would make the following suggestion. Political philosophy is within Christianity as the line is within the circle, as our erotic search for perfection is within the completeness of the whole. Socrates' death is an icon of perfection, whereas Christ's was complete.

These remarks may serve as an introduction to a question that has emerged on occasion in this paper, namely Grant's relationship to the "gnostic saint" Simone Weil and to what might paradoxically be called gnostic Christianity or Christian gnosticism. The term is paradoxical because the gnostic elements in Christianity were more or less purged by the early Church Fathers. They were purged, moreover, for the very good philosophical reason that they tended to disrupt the balance of existence symbolized, for example, by St. Augustine's image of the Christian as a pilgrim directed towards the Heavenly City. Whether activist or contemplative, gnostics in antiquity and gnostics in modernity have sought to escape reality. In Christian language, they sought to escape God's creation. Characteristically, ancient gnostics devised spiritual formulae to transfigure their own consciousness into the imaginative contemplation of the beyond; modern gnostics have typically taken a short-cut and sought to "change the world," as Marx put it, so that it conformed to their own libidinal fantasies. Either way, the gnostic escape is simply evidence of a hatred of reality as given. In Christian language, gnostics hate creation and, more radically, they hate the Creator.

This line of thought had an obvious appeal to Grant. To begin with, it was spiritually serious and demanding in the same way that Hegel ensured that his readers considered the world very seriously. But second, as Zdravko Planinc suggested, when one thinks about what technology is, one attempts to understand its status as a being, its "ontological status." This is indicated by a negative response to the question: can one love technology? Because one cannot love technology one wonders: what is it? Or rather, what is the spirituality that is expressed in or through technology? Grant has indicated several times that the answer is to be found in Nietzsche. More precisely, in *The Will to Power* Nietzsche provided the following description:

> ...we shall conquer and come to power even without truth. The charm that works for us, the Venus eye that fascinates even our opponents, and blinds them, is the magic of the extreme, the seductive force that radiates from all that is utmost: we immoralists are the utmost.[68]

To put the matter very summarily indeed: the question that lay behind Grant's thinking concerned the status of modernity and of technology within modernity. For Grant, technology is our fate and modernity is our destiny. At times, modernity and technology must have seemed to him to have exhaustively symbolized reality as given. It was at these times that the gnostic appeals of Simone Weil's speculations may have been strongest. She may have suggested to Grant a *gnosis* of escape from technology through meditation and thereby also modernity and even from reality.

Saint Augustine has indicated that sin involves more than temptation. All the children of Adam and Eve are tempted. Sin also involves delectation and then assent, which is to say we actively participate in the acts of sin. George Grant may well have been tempted by the gnosticism of Simone Weil; one may even say that he took a kind of delight in escaping, perhaps with the aid of Mozart, from the ugliness and spiritual dessication of technological modernity. He did not, however, assent to the inanition of the soul that a serious gnostic search entails. Grant remained a thinker, one who engaged in meditation upon the urgent present of society. Not, indeed, to change it but to understand it.

In a companion article in this volume Michael Gillespie concludes that Grant was a Christian moral philosopher, which is not a terribly misleading characterization, but also that he paid insufficient attention to differences in the nature of regimes, underestimating thereby what divides Americanism, communism, and national socialism. It is true that one of Grant's voices, which might be called the voice of the Loyalist heartland, is critical of the United States and indicates that the American version of the technological society overseas is often friendly towards tyrannical regimes. What such observations indicate, I believe, is that the concept of regime may not be so fundamental a category of analysis as we are accustomed to believe. Or, to put it another way, Grant may be understood to have argued that the technological society is itself a kind of regime for which liberal and tyrannical governments are variants. In any event, the careful attention Grant paid to the detail of American government and its impact on Canada was, I believe, more evidence of a robust common sense. But common sense is not necessarily of assistance in resisting the temptations of a gnostic saint. One reason why Grant was able to retain a balanced consciousness may be that he found what he was looking for in the work of Leo Strauss. The revival of political philosophy was indeed a blessing, both for Grant and for his readers.

NOTES

1 Leo Strauss, "What is Political Philosophy," *What is Political Philosophy*. (Glencoe,Illinois: The Free Press, 1959), p.10.

2 Ibid., pp. 93-94.

3 George Grant, "Nietzsche and the Ancients," *Technology and Justice*. (Toronto: House of Anansi Press Limited, 1986), p. 92.

4   Grant, *Lament for a Nation — The Defeat of Canadian Nationalism*. (Ottawa: Carleton University Press, 1989), p. 96.

5   Grant, *Technology and Empire — Perspectives on North America*. (Toronto: House of Anansi Press Limited, 1969), p. 11.

6   See Joan E. O'Donovan, *George Grant and the Twilight of Justice*. (Toronto: University of Toronto Press, 1984), pp. 10-11; O'Donovan, "The Battleground of Liberalism: Politics of Eternity and Time," *The Chesterton Review* (11:1985), pp. 131-54; Frank K. Flinn, "George Parkin Grant: A Bibliographical Introduction," in Larry Schmidt, ed., *George Grant in Process: Essays and Conversations*. (Toronto: House of Anansi Press Limited, 1978), pp. 195-99; Flinn, "George Grant's Three Languages," *The Chesterton Review*, (11:1985), pp. 155-66.

7   Grant, "Tyranny and Wisdom," *Technology and Empire*, p. 86.

8   Grant, "Religion and the State," op.cit.*supra*, p. 44.

9   Friedrich Nietzsche, "On Scholars," *Thus Spoke Zarathustra*, in Walter Kaufmann, *The Portable Nietzsche*. (New York: The Viking Press, 1868), p. 236.

10   Ibid.

11   Ibid., pp. 236-237.

12   Ibid., p. 237.

13   Ibid.

14   Ibid.

15   Ibid.

16   Ibid., p. 238.

17   Ibid.

18   "The Teaching of Philosophy in Canada," *Encyclopedia Canadiana*. (Toronto: The Grolier Society of Canada, 1958), 8:183.

19   Ibid.

20   Ibid., p. 184.

21   Ibid.

22   Grant, "Philosophy in Canada," *Royal Commission on National Development*, Royal Commission Studies (Ottawa: King's Printer, 1951), p. 119.

23   Ibid.

24   Ibid., p. 132.

25   July 16-17, 1988. William Christian, "George Grant and Religion," forthcoming in *Saturday Night Magazine*.

26   Friedrich Nietzsche, *Beyond Good and Evil — Prelude to a Philosophy of the Future*, transl. by Walter Kaufmann. (New York: Vintage Books, 1966) Sec. 211, p. 136.

27   Ibid.

28   *Meno*, transl. by W.R.M. Lamb, Loeb Classical Library, No. 166. (Cambridge, Massachusetts: Harvard University Press, 1983), 80E.

29   Plato, *Charmides*, in *Charmides, Alcibiades, Hipparchus, The Lovers, Theages, Minos and Epinomis*, transl. by W.R.M. Lamb, Loeb Classic Library, No. 163. (Cambridge, Massachusetts: Harvard University Press, 1982), 165b-c.

30   Grant, "Philosophy," op.cit.*supra*, p. 133.

31   Eric Voegelin, *The New Science of Politics*. (Chicago: University of Chicago Press, 1952), pp. 1-2.

32   Grant, *English-Speaking Justice*. (Sackville: Mount Allison University Press, 1974), p. 1.

33   Grant, *Philosophy in the Mass Age*. (Toronto: Copp Clark Publishing, 1959), p. ix.

34   Ibid., p. iii.

35   Ibid.

36   Ibid.

37   Ibid.

38   Ibid., p. iv.

39   Ibid.

40   Ibid.

41   Ibid.

42   Ibid.

43   Ibid.

44   Ibid., p. v.

45   Ibid.

46   Ibid., pp. v-vi.

47   Ibid.

48   Ibid., p. vii.

49   Ibid., pp. vi-vii.

50   Ibid., p. vii. Grant did not indicate what he meant by "the western Christian doctrine of providence." In Technology and Empire, p. 44, he attributed certain defects in one of his essays to the fact that he "could not face the fact that we were living at the end of western Christianity." One more familiar with Grant's religious convictions, for which there is little enough published evidence, might find a suitable challenge in the explication of this problem.

51   Ibid.

52   Ibid.

53   Ibid.

54   Ibid., p. viii.

55   Ibid.

56   See Emil Fackenheim, "Would Hegel Today be a Hegelian?" in Dialogue, 9:2 (1970), 222-6; and the response by James A. Doull, Grant's colleague at Dalhousie, pp. 226-35.

57   Grant, *Philosophy in the Mass Age*, p. viii.

58   Ibid.

59   Ibid.

60   Ibid., p. ix.

61   Reprinted in Grant, *Technology and Empire*, pp. 79-109.

62   Strauss, *The City and Man*. (Chicago: The University of Chicago Press, 1964), p. 1.

63   Strauss, *Liberalism: Ancient and Modern*. (New York: Basic Books, 1968), p. 24.

64   William Christian, op.cit.*supra*.

65 Ibid.

66 Grant, "Tyranny and Wisdom," p. 109.

67 Grant, "Faith and the Multiversity," *Technology and Justice*, p. 72.

68 Friedrich Nietzsche, *The Will to Power*, transl. by Walter Kaufmann. (New York: Random House, 1968), Sec. 749, p. 396. See Eric Voegelin, "Wisdom and the Magic of the Extreme," *Southern Review*, N.S.17 (1981), pp. 235-287.

GEORGE GRANT AND THE TRADITION OF
POLITICAL PHILOSOPHY

Michael Allen Gillespie

The work of George Grant is associated with what has been called the revival of political philosophy. This revival was in large part a reaction to the unexpected re-emergence of political fanaticism in the twentieth century, and was particularly strong in North America under the leadership of Leo Strauss, Eric Voegelin, and Hannah Arendt. These thinkers, in disparate ways, resurrected political philosophy from the sepulchre of intellectual history and re-established it as an important part of political science.

The revival of political philosophy, however, was dependent upon the antecedent revival of philosophy brought about by Friederich Nietzsche and Martin Heidegger. Since Hegel, thinkers of various stripes have proclaimed the end of philosophy. Hegel himself argued that philosophy had come to an end because the love of wisdom had given way to wisdom itself in the form of absolute knowledge and science. In his view everything of any real importance had finally become accessible to human reason, in large part because the world had revealed itself to be nothing other than human reason. Hegel argued that all of the traditional metaphysical questions of ontology, logic, theology, cosmology, and anthropology could be answered through an investigation of human consciousness and history. Moreover, he was convinced that he had completed such an investigation. In the political realm this meant that all of the principles of justice had been finally and fully determined and that it only remained to implement them. The idea of progress that so dominated the later nineteenth century seemed to suggest that such an implementation was inevitable.

Nietzsche was the first thinker to question this conclusion seriously. Like the Romantics before him he was deeply concerned with the subconscious and subrational grounds of consciousness and reason, and he tried to show that these grounds had not been comprehended in previous thought. In his view, the failure of modern thinking to come to terms with this irrational element at its core was a reflection of reason's conceited belief that, in understanding itself, it understood everything. Nietzsche's critique of modern philosophy opened up a new horizon for thinking, and thus for philosophizing. This led Heidegger and others to conclude that while traditional philosophy might be at an end, this end in fact only represented a radiant new beginning, and thus a unique opportunity for original thinking.

The general public trust in progress and enlightenment, however, remained unshaken, and it was really only the horrors of World War One and the emergence of Bolshevism and Fascism that shattered this faith. The fundamental questions of politics, the questions of justice, freedom, and political order, again came to the fore. Moreover, the failure of "revived" philosophy to explain or deal with these political questions and the actual complicity of the new thinking in these disasters, indicated the need not merely for philosophy, but for a philosophy that began with politics, or at least took politics seriously. Strauss, Voegelin and Arendt found such a political philosophy in ancient thought. The revival of political philosophy was thus also the revival of ancient political philosophy.

This revival took place largely within the horizon established by the revival of philosophy in general. Both Strauss and Arendt, for example, were students of Heidegger. Thus, Grant's place within the revival of political philosophy is comprehensible only on the basis of his position within this larger philosophical revival, for he is deeply influenced by it. Grant, however like Voegelin, Strauss and Arendt, was also suspicious of the antipolitical essence of the thought of Nietzsche and Heidegger, although his doubts were never as great as theirs. While he was sympathetic to Nietzsche's and Heidegger's analyses of modern society, he also distanced himself from some of their conclusions. Therefore, in order to place Grant's thought, it is necessary to delineate his position at the juncture and disjuncture of the revived philosophy and political philosophy.

As Barry Cooper points out in his contribution to this volume, Hegel was the pre-eminent philosophical influence on Grant in his early work, and especially in *Philosophy in the Mass Age*. Grant admired not merely Hegel's synthesis of Greek and Christian elements, but also his synthesis of the doctrine of freedom propagated by the Enlightenment and modern science. If Hegel was correct, then North America in Grant's view was heir to the whole of the human tradition, and the place where Hegel's rational state could come to its fullest perfection. Grant, however, was unable to sustain this hopeful early view; his more mature thought was characterized by a deepening reassessment of Hegel in light of what he saw as the failure of North American society to produce the human excellence that Hegel had predicted.

For Grant, this realization resulted, apparently, from his practical and thoughtful experience of everyday life, which led him to recognize what he so elegantly expressed in *Lament for a Nation*: that the cosmopolitanism of Hegel's universal state undermines the attachment to one's own that is essential to all human excellence. Evidently, this recognition was in part a reflection of his deeply religious stance towards life. In his report to the Massey Commission Grant asserts, in a manner reminiscent of Simone Weil, that "the study of philosophy is the analysis of the traditions of our society and the judgement of those traditions against our varying intuitions of the Perfection of God."[1] Against these standards the liberal and cosmopolitan life of North America did not, in Grant's view, measure up. Grant found a philosophical explanation for this failure in Nietzsche's critique of modern society, in the idea of technology as it was articulated by Martin Heidegger, in Jacques Ellul, a thinker who was deeply influenced by Heidegger.[2]

For Heidegger, technology is the name for the modern destiny of Being, which establishes man as the ground of all being and aims at the universal mastery and subjugation of nature.[3] In Heidegger's view this process begins with the establishment of man-as-subject in the thought of Descartes, and is achieved by the transformation of every traditional thing into a mere object for the subject. This process of objectification secures the subject in the midst of becoming, first by the re-creation of the world as a representation within the human imagination, but then in practice, by the application of human labour which reworks nature itself into an image of this world-picture.[4] This modern project initially seems to aim at the preservation and enhancement of man but in Heidegger's view this is an illusion, for technology is not a tool that humanity employs for ends of its own, but a sending or destiny of Being that uses not merely the natural world but man himself to achieve its ends. In this respect, Heidegger's analysis of technology is similar to Marx's analysis of the role of capital in modern society. Thus the hegemony of technology ends not in human well-being but in human degradation. Man himself becomes objectified, becomes a mere object of use, a part of the standing reserve whose only purpose is the further development of global technology. This techno-logical impulse leads to the universal and ultimately totalitarian organization of modern man. Heidegger thus concludes that Ameri-canism, communism, and Nazism are identical when viewed from a metaphysical perspective, that they are all merely forms of modern subjectivity that aim at the dreary, universal organization of the common man.[5] Technology becomes such an all-encompassing des-tiny for him that it renders all other distinctions irrelevant. To Heidegger, for example, the production of corpses at Auschwitz is in essence indistinguishable from the production of fertilizer at a chemical plant. The moral differences in this example become superfluous.

Grant draws heavily on Heidegger's analysis but does not always accept Heidegger's conclusions. For Grant modern society and modern politics are thoroughly determined by technology. Liberal-ism, he argues, is merely the civil theology of technological society, a theology of technique that debases the notion of human excellence and degrades man. He follows Heidegger and Ellul quite faithfully in this respect. In light of what he saw as the technological essence of Ameri-can empire revealed in the Vietnam war, Grant even repeats Heidegger's assertion that Americanism, communism, and Nazism are identical.

Confronted with this destiny of technology, which in Grant's view, poses a supreme danger to man's human being, Grant suggests two different solutions. The first is a practical or "lived" alternative that derives from his experience of life in a small, close-knit commu-nity; the second is a more theoretical alternative that arises out of his participation in the revival of political philosophy.

On the most fundamental level Grant is not a systematic thinker. He admits, for example, changing his mind on certain funda-mental questions. His thinking is united not by a single principle or doctrine but by a particular way of life. He draws upon the thought of others but he does not synthesize it into a new whole. Rather, each borrowing serves more as a spotlight that reveals some aspect of the kind of life he wants to defend. In this sense his analysis and critique of technology is not merely a rejection of modern cosmopolitanism, but a defence of the traditions of the local life that is the home and ground of ethical life. As Cooper points out, Grant sees the tradition of technology as repudiating rather than sanctifying the past. For Grant we must rather become "miners of the buried past,"[6] that is, of a past that has not yet been obliterated by the modern liberal-cosmopolitan-technological impulse.

This solution to the problem of technology, however, is not altogether unique to Grant. Indeed here, too, Grant knowingly or unknowingly follows Heidegger who, in his later thought and especially in his critique of technology, turned to the local community and its ethos as the true home of man and the place of ethical life. What is characteristic of both Heidegger and Grant, in this respect, is a loss of faith in the political dimension of human existence. To both, political life seems to be all too fully determined and subsumed by the force of technology. Politics thus appears to be thoroughly determined by more fundamental social forces.

This view of the relationship between society and politics puts Grant at odds with the general tenor of the revival of political philosophy. This is particularly important because Grant relies upon one of the leaders of this revival, Leo Strauss, in formulating his second alternative to the hegemony of technology. The revival of political philosophy in the hands of Strauss and, to a lesser extent, Arendt is certainly indebted to the thought of Martin Heidegger. But it is also in essence a profound critique of Heidegger which, drawing upon ancient thought, seeks to demonstrate the continuing relevance and, in a sense, pre-eminence of the political. Like Heidegger, Strauss recognized the important role that technology played in shaping modern life; but in contrast to Heidegger, he did not believe that it was finally decisive in determining the character of the political realm. Political life, in his view, is not simply epiphenomenal, not merely subservient to or a reflection of an underlying social reality. Rather, political science properly understood is the master science. Society and technology only come to predominate because of an explicit though little recognized decision by early modern political philosophers that these forces ought to predominate, as the inevitable result of a self-abnegation of responsibility by political philosophy. It is this self-abnegation of responsibility, Strauss argues, which lies at the heart of the modern natural rights teaching that is the essence of liberalism. Liberalism, thus understood, is an essentially hedonistic doctrine that aims not at virtue or goodness but at preservation, a liberation of the passions, and a pleasurable life.

Grant draws upon this element of Strauss's thought and conflates it with Heidegger's critique of modernity as technology. In Strauss, Grant discovers the political element that is lacking in Heidegger and Nietzsche. Strauss's analysis of liberalism as the liberation of the passions provides Grant with a political explanation for the advent of the technological imperative that Heidegger describes. This amalgamation of Strauss and Heidegger, however, depends upon a one-sided reading that fastens upon Strauss' critique of modern natural-rights teaching and the arid modern liberalism it conveys, but fails to grasp the qualifications that Strauss places upon this critique and the decisive way in which he distinguishes himself from Heidegger. Heidegger and Strauss cannot be brought together as easily as Grant imagines.

For Heidegger, technology is not merely a modern problem, but rather the final result of the revelation of Being that began with the pre-Socratics and that was given its decisive form by Plato and Aristotle. Strauss believes that Heidegger too easily dismisses ancient political philosophy and fails to recognize the extent to which the triumph of technology flows from particular decisions by early modern thinkers. For Strauss, the political must be taken more seriously; the failure to do so leads to disaster. Heidegger himself, in Strauss's view, is an example of the consequences of failing to take politics seriously. In his pursuit of a suprapolitical solution to the problem of technology Heidegger becomes entangled in the most heinous and abysmal politics of the modern age, the politics of Nazism.

Thus to understand the crisis of modernity properly, it is necessary to understand it as an essentially political crisis; and we can only understand it in this way by holding it against the broader backdrop of ancient political philosophy. What is central for Strauss, and almost entirely absent in Grant, is the importance of the nature of the regime. Strauss believes that this key element of ancient thought is of decisive importance in understanding modernity as well. He thus disagrees fundamentally with Heidegger's and Grant's identification of Americanism, communism, and Nazism. Such an identification fails to distinguish the differences between the regimes that remain salient and indeed decisive and those that don't. Under the influence of Heidegger and Ellul, Grant comes to overestimate vastly the power of a technologically-guided social science employing propaganda, polling, and so on, to subvert and subordinate all contemporary politics. He thus does not sufficiently appreciate the continuing importance of the political.

What Grant is attracted to in ancient political philosophy is not so much its teaching about the relationship of the social and the political as its awareness of the eternal which, as Strauss points out, modernity sacrifices in its attempt to become the master and possessor of nature.[7] Grant thus admires the way the ancients understood their mortality in terms of the eternity of nature or the gods, the manner in which they grasped their own past in terms of this eternity as a tradition rather than as history, and the notion of human excellence that was developed by Plato in his portrayal of Socrates. None of these aspects of antiquity, however, is especially political, although each finds its echo in Grant's religious stance and his defence of localism and parochialism.

Grant thus tries to mark out a position between Heidegger on the one hand and Strauss on the other, a position that relies on both but accepts neither. It is unclear whether such a position is philosophically defensible. It is difficult to see, for example, how he can consistently adopt the Heideggerian analysis of modern society as technology, without accepting Heidegger's conclusion that moral differences are relatively insignificant in the face of technological uniformity, when it is clear from Grant's opposition to abortion and euthanasia that such a conclusion is anathema to him. It is also hard to understand how he can combine the thought of Strauss and Heidegger without distorting the meaning of one or the other, since they take such opposing views of the importance of the political.

Perhaps it is most fruitful to understand Grant not as a philosopher nor as a political philosopher in the revivalistic sense we have employed here, but as a moral philosopher and, indeed, as a Christian moral philosopher. He shows himself clearly as such in the connection he makes, in a manner much at odds with that of Strauss, between Socrates and Christ. He describes himself as "a political philosopher within Christianity."[8] One can be reasonably sure that it is such a moral stance that enables him to reject the more extreme and unpalatable conclusions that are seen by thinkers like Heidegger as the necessary and inevitable consequences of an analysis of modern society as technology. For Grant there is an unchangeable point of reference, an idea of perfection or God. Thus, he sees man not as infinitely malleable, as Nietzsche and Heidegger suggest, but as a creature of God. In a similar way he can find grounds for his praise of the local community as the home of human excellence. Whether and to what extent such a moral position can challenge the comprehensive philosophical vision of Heidegger and the profound political philosophic endeavour of Strauss depends upon the capacity of this moral philosophy to locate and defend a ground of its own that can consistently encompass both Heidegger and Strauss, without falling prey to either. While Grant's thought at times seems unequal to this task, his character is a sort of representation of this position in the flesh. It will be left to others to try to defend it in theory.

NOTES

[1] Grant, "Philosophy," in Canada, *Royal Commission on National Development*, Royal Commission Studies. (Ottawa: King's Printer, 1951), pp. 119, 132.

[2] For Grant's view of the importance of Nietzsche see *Time as History*, (Toronto: Canadian Broadcasting Corporation, 1969) and "Nietzsche and the Ancients: Philosophy and Scholarship," in *Technology and Justice* (Toronto: House of Anansi Press Limited, 1986). Grant's debt to Heidegger is in a sense much deeper than his debt to Nietzsche but also much less fully acknowledged. To anyone familiar with the work of Heidegger and Ellul Grant's debt will be readily apparent. On his debt to Ellul see *Philosophy in the Mass Age* (Toronto: Copp Clark Publishing, 1959), p. ix.

[3] On Heidegger's analysis of technology see his *Technik und die Kehre* (Pfullingen: Neske, 1976) and his "Ansprache zur Heimatabend," in *700 Jahre Messkirch* (Messkirch: n.p., 1969).

4   Martin Heidegger, *Nietzsche,* 2 vols. (Pfullingen: Neske, 1961), 2:141-92; "Die Zeit des Weltbilds", in *Holzwege* (Frankfurt am Main: Klostermann, 1950).

5   Heidegger, "Nur ein Gott Kann uns retten," *Der Spiegel,* no. 23 (1976), 206; *Platons Lehre von der Wahrheit. Mit einem Brief uber den "Humanismus"* (Bern: Francke, 1947), 88-89; "Dankansprache," in *Ansprachen zum 80. Geburtstag 1969 in Messkirch* (Messkirch: n.p., 1969), p. 34.

6   Grant, *Philosophy in the Mass Age,* p. v.

7   Grant, *Time as History,* p. 48.

8   Grant, "Nietzsche and the Ancients," *Technology and Justice.* (Toronto: House of Anansi Press Limited, 1986), p. 92.

PART IV

THE POSSIBILITIES OF A RELIGIOUS LIFE

LAW, LOVE AND THE COMMON GOOD

Joan O'Donovan

It is obvious to anyone who has read with equal openness all parts of *Lament for a Nation* that its legacy encompasses even as overtly theological a topic as the present one, for Grant plainly declares here that Canada's persisting political integrity has depended historically — and still depends — on the continuing public articulation of two Christian conservatisms: those of French-Canadian Catholicism and British Loyalist Anglicanism. In their common commitment to an individual and collective "ethic of self-restraint," maintained socially by a "high degree of law," Grant finds the *raison d'être* of Canada's separate political existence in North America.[1] This indigenous tradition of virtue is what makes Canadian nationhood worthy of loyalty, protection, and, indeed, lament. Its recollection renders the attachment of Canadians to their political past an act of patriotism rather than nostalgia, by setting the object of their particular affection in relation to the universal common good.

Yet there is a double irony in Grant's lament for the vanishing of this tradition. The more evident irony is that most present-day defenders of Canada's independent political identity are unable to recollect their country's historic rationale. The minority strands of romantic nationalism and anti-corporate socialism are equally cut off from Canada's founding conservatisms. Less evident, but of greater theoretical consequence, is the political inadequacy of these foundations themselves. It is to this that Grant directs us when, in his introduction to the Carleton Library edition of *Lament*, he remarks on "the romanticism of the original dream."[2] While he reproaches his own "failure in irony" for writing what "many simple people... took... to be... a lament for the passing of a British dream of Canada,"[3] his reproach really falls on the simple-mindedness of his readers. For his *Lament* discloses to the attentive eye the insufficiency of the dominant strand of Canada's fundamental conservatism, that is, the British Loyalist strand. (Writing as a participant in the English-speaking political tradition, Grant declines to pronounce judgement on the French-speaking counterpart.) In short, the insufficiency of British Loyalist conservatism lies in the traditionalism inherited from its parent conservatism. As British conservatism was "less a clear view of existence than an appeal to an ill-defined past," so Loyalist conservatism "was no better defined than a kind of suspicion that we in Canada could be less lawless and have a greater sense of propriety than the United States."[4]

The essence of traditionalism is the allegiance to long-accepted social forms and proprieties without an articulate conception of the moral and spiritual ends they serve. It is the disproportionate love of the *authority* of human law as distinct from its *content*, entailing an exaggerated estimation of the accomplishment of the law as such. Just this overestimation of political institutions has characterised British conservatism from Hooker to Burke, notwithstanding Hooker's practically unlimited confidence in the Law of Reason, which spared him the inarticulateness of most traditionalism.

This last observation suggests a further irony that Grant does not draw out. Typically, he links the political ineffectualness of eighteenth-century British conservatism to the ascendency of the doctrines of Locke, Smith and Hume, arguing that the Loyalists' inheritance was a mixture of minority conservative and majority liberal elements. Right from Canada's inception, the legacy of Hooker was being submerged beneath the new wave of moral and political science. (Memorable for its incisive wit is Grant's portrait of "the educated among the Loyalists" as "that extraordinary concoction, straight Locke with a dash of Anglicanism.")[5] What he leaves unexamined are the theological weaknesses of Hooker's establishment Anglicanism, which make it in the long run an inadequate Christian political tradition.

I am not primarily interested in offering a theological criticism of Hooker, but rather in clarifying essential aspects of a Christian theory of law in relation to love and to the common good. Such a theory gathers up for reflection the possibilities of the Christian life. (My theological viewpoint does, however, imply criticism of Hooker's, which I shall touch on briefly in response to Grant's appeal to his conservative legacy.) I have made law the subject of theological consideration for three reasons. In the first place, I regard the absence of sound Christian thought about law in liberal technological society as a critical feature of the modern dilemma that Grant has unfolded so penetratingly. Even when it intends to subject the prevailing ethos to the judgement of faith, contemporary Christian theology frequently subjects faith to the judgement of the prevailing ethos on understandings of law that might effectively oppose it. This is so of the currently influential German Protestant theology indebted especially to the writings of Jurgen Moltmann, which seeks to criticise liberal ideology from a radically eschatological theological viewpoint. Such an eschatological polemic against contemporary ideology unwittingly colludes with it in dismissing pre-modern theological doctrines of law connected with God's creation, providential ordering, and sanctification of the world. I would argue that re-articulation rather than rejection of these doctrines is the more effective theological antidote to the degenerative ailments of our society.

In the second place, the search for an adequate theological conception of law, undertaken in full consciousness of modern potentialities, is a continuous concern in Grant's own thought. This concern is most explicitly developed in *Philosophy in the Mass Age* where, under the sway of Hegel's historical self-confidence, he formulates the principles of an absolute morality compatible with the modern awareness of freedom. This morality incorporates a twofold understanding of law as unconditional limit "of which we do not take the measure, but by which we ourselves are measured and defined,"[6] and as binding necessity which "carries evil within itself" and "is the very negation of freedom and power... ."[7] While nowhere else does Grant attempt a comparably systematic treatment of the subject of law, nevertheless the ideas of limit and necessity pervade his subsequent theological-ethical reflections on the themes of love, knowledge, justice and goodness. Indeed, his late reworked essay, "Faith and the Multiversity," included in the most recent collection of his writings, *Technology and Justice* (1986), is an unsurpassed clarification of concepts that illuminate the subject of law. At the same time, these concepts are insufficiently — or questionably — developed from a theological standpoint, in part because of Grant's continuing dependence on the Christian gnosticism of Simone Weil.

This brings us to the third reason for focusing on law: namely, Grant's theoretical weakness, or incompleteness, in this area, which makes a theological contribution at this point worthwhile. Regrettably, this paper will not make the contribution called for by the excellence of Grant's own immense intellectual effort, and so must be regarded as a minor token of my esteem and admiration for his life's work.

Bearing in mind Grant's own theoretical concerns, we shall address ourselves to two broad, theological interests within the exceedingly complex sphere of law. The first relates to the role of law in created order and investigates the concepts of natural law and natural teleology. It also includes the relationship of natural law to the positive law of political communities. The second relates to the role of law in the sanctification of believers, directing our attention to the evangelical law of the Church. With respect to both of these theological interests, in creation law and in the evangelical law, we shall place in the foreground the unity of law and love that is so fundamental to Grant's own thought.

Law and Love in Created Order

> ... it may perhaps be said negatively that what has been absent for us is the affirmation of a possible apprehension of the world beyond that as a field of objects considered as pragmata — an apprehension present not only in its height as 'theory' but as the undergirding of our loves and friendships, of our arts and reverences, and indeed as the setting for our dealing with the objects of the human and non-human world. Perhaps we are lacking the recognition that our response to the whole should not most deeply be that of doing, nor even that of terror and anguish, but that of wondering or marvelling at what is, being amazed or astonished by it, or perhaps best, in a discarded English usage, admiring it; and that such a stance, as beyond all bargains and conveniences, is the only source from which purposes may be manifest for our necessary calculating.[8]

There is no more beautiful and arresting expression in Grant's writings of the dependence of human moral community on a primal relationship of man to himself, and to the non-human world in which love and law are indissolubly wedded. Against the loveless totality of technological mastery, in which is united the absolute and purposeless freedom of men and the absolute and purposeless determinism of nature, Grant sets the totality available to men's admiring contemplation, which undergirds their manifold loves with an unconditional, constraining claim ("as beyond all bargains and conveniences"). Only in loving surrender to this totality can men find purposes for their technical calculations. Outside of this stance they cannot invent (in the archaic sense of "come upon" — from the Latin *invenire*) the common good, in the service of which alone their inventions (in the modern sense of "fabrications") receive sufficient justification. Without this fundamental receptivity, described in Grant's later writings as "consent to the fact [of] authentic otherness,"[9] they are shut out from the individual and communal practice of justice as the rendering to each being of its due. It is essential to note that Grant does not deny to us moderns this "apprehension of the world," but rather its common "affirmation."

From a Christian theological point of view, the Biblical doctrine of creation offers the truest and most complete affirmation of this "apprehension". For it situates the human community in a totality of lawful order established and sustained by the loving will of its creator. As God's love, even in His creation of the world, has as its ultimate object the perfection and goodness of His being, so the finite beings created by His love have as their final end participation in His goodness. Thus, to apprehend the finite being in its goodness is to apprehend it as a finite participation in the divine perfection. Moreover, this apprehension is always and necessarily of a finite form, the form of the creature being the mode of its participation in God's goodness, and, hence, the determination of its immanent goodness. Thus, there is expressed in the biblical vision of creation a double teleology: a double directedness of every creature to God as its transcendent end, and to the perfection of its form as its immanent end. The psalmist's declaration that "the heavens are telling the glory of God; and the firmament proclaims his handiwork" (Ps. 19:1) stands together with the testimony of Genesis 1 that God has populated the waters and dry land under the firmament with diverse creatures "according to their kinds." The term "kinds," synonymous with "species," denotes the ontological equivalence among creatures of similar substantial forms that constitutes a bond of unity and, thus, an element of cosmological order. The substantial form of the creature is also the basis of a third, ontologically dependent teleology: that which unifies distinct kinds by ordering the good of one kind to the good of another. This is the teleological hierarchy of Genesis 1:28-30, established by God's allocating of seed-bearing plants and fruit-bearing trees for man's food, and all green plants to feed other warm- and cold-blooded animals. But it is also the non-hierarchical, co-operative interaction of kinds that maintains the stability of created order, commonly referred to as "the balance of nature." A complete theological articulation of the goodness of finite beings and of the totality to which they belong includes this whole complex of generic and teleological relationships.[10]

In the biblical account of creation, purpose and law are intimately connected. The primary connection, it should be emphasized, is the sovereign will of God who brings forth the elements of natural order by His commands, so that the substantial forms in their cosmic relationships are divine decrees. The finite nature, therefore, is a law not only in the Aristotelian sense of controlling principle of action, but in the basic theological sense of being divinely legislated. Only as the expression of God's bountiful love is created nature itself a law of love, to be accepted and obeyed joyfully. Only as the communication of God's superabundant being is created nature a law of perfection and completeness, to be admired and extolled. Only as the object of God's unchanging and certain knowledge is created nature a law of truth, to be submitted to in the act of knowing. Of course, the teleology of created nature by no means exhausts the lawfulness of the whole. At the level of matter imperceptible to the naked senses — the molecular, atomic, and sub-atomic levels — where matter becomes chemistry and energy, and order abstract algebraic and symbolic equations, lawfulness is (for us!) non-teleological necessity, even if stated in the language of indeterminacy and probability.[11] While the Biblical authors know nothing of this scientifically established necessity, it is, nevertheless, comprehended in their belief in God's sovereign disposition of all temporal and spatial being, order and movement, and as such, is not without goodness and perfection.

The affirmation of created order has weighty implications for man's relationship to himself and to the non-human world. First, with regard to his quest for knowledge of human and non-human objects, it means chiefly that he can never abandon sensible knowledge of individual forms and the conceptions of "nature" and "substance" associated with it. For "substance" denotes the inner, active unity of the individual which integrates the composite structures and processes entailed in its being. In its intelligibility as essence or nature, the substance situates the individual within the finite network of generic and teleological relationships, binding it to the goodness and intelligibility of the whole. Thus it is that any theoretical account of the whole which claims to refute the "hypothesis" of substance, denying the integrity of individuals, along with their generic and teleological ordering, is incompatible with the Christian affirmation of creation. In the light of this affirmation, the theologian must insist that true knowledge of, for instance, a maple tree, involves the fundamental natural divisions between non-living and living, vegetable and animal substances, and, in this case, the generic, specific and sub-specific divisions within the vegetable nature. Knowledge of what the maple tree is, in the first place, of its immanent end or purpose and is attained by our reflection on its characteristic, perceptible operations: of standing, growing, producing, and shedding seasonal foliage. As the beauty and goodness of the maple are given in our naive experience of its determinate being, its individual form, so, in our reflective knowledge, the concepts of goodness and perfection are inseparable from those of its nature and end. Upon our grasp of its immanent *telos* depends our knowledge of the maple's secondary purposes: as providing anchorage for soil, food for insects, shelter and homes for birds and animals, wood for human use, and an aesthetic object in the culturally contrived landscape of the garden.

In regard to our action towards the maple tree and other natural objects, it is just this relationship of primary to secondary *tele* that determines its proper order and limits. Even in respect of non-human natures, human purposes for them are bound by the divine decree that they are goods in themselves before they are goods for others. The primary *telos* of a natural substance is a constraint on human action that can never be simply disregarded. In the case of the maple tree this is the individual actualization of its specific "maple" form, its flourishing as a maple tree. While in the secondary hierarchy of natures the good of the maple tree is subservient to the good of humankind, such that man's uses for it occasionally justify destruction of its substantial form, nevertheless the created good of the maple's immanent form places limits on man's right to consume it in use.

This balance between man's right to use nature for human purposes and his obligation to respect it by letting it be and assisting its preservation, is a constant mark of his relationship to non-human creatures. It is the form of his divinely-granted lordship over creation (Genesis 1:26-8), as Genesis 2 reveals by placing Adam in the Garden of Eden with the vocation of tending it (2:15). Adam's work of tending the garden is as conducive to the admiring contemplation and nurturing of the vegetable world as to consumptive use of it. It is the first couple's rebellion against God that vitiates this proper balance in their rule over creation. Their exile from the Garden is at once an alienation flowing inexorably from their violation of divinely-ordained limits, and a divine expulsion, God's free judgement on their evil-doing.

The exile of the human community is a rupture of created order wherein the chief bond of unity between mankind and the rest of the creation — namely, mutual conformity to God's will — is broken. The result is a struggle for domination between human and non-human nature in which man is both master and slave, tyrant and idolater.[12] He idolatrously enslaves himself to the natural elements, likewise in primitive nature worship and in the reductionist ideologies of modern science, only to gain manipulative mastery over them, whether by magical or technological methods.

By contrast, man's proper lordship over creation is exercised within creation, within the divinely established totality of individuals, relationships and wholes, of teleological and generic orderings. Its exercise is enmeshed in the consciousness that man too is a creaturely substance ordered to immanent and transcendent ends by means of manifold activities, each of which is subject to internal and external laws and limits. His thought is ordered to the knowledge of God and of the world in its dependence on Him; his free will, to obedience to the divine command, his desire to the possession of infinite and finite goods in their right relationship; his speech, to the communication of truth; his work, to the sustenance and enrichment of human life by the unfolding of the creation's proper potentialities; and his communal life, to the common good. With respect to the sexual community of marriage, the common good is the mutual fidelity, communion and support of the partners and the procreation of children. With respect to the more inclusive civic community, the common good is the natural justice laid down, according to centuries of ecclesiastical tradition, by Christ's law of neighbourly love which commands that "whatever you wish that men would do to you, do so to them."[13] Only in and through these divinely-given ends and laws does man's creaturely activity achieve integrity and fulfillment. They are the objective conditions of moral life that, notwithstanding their objectivity, forever elude the objectification of human knowledge, being prior and transcendent to the willing and knowing of individuals, and susceptible of being apprehended by means of participation alone.

It is in relation to this natural order of created goods that political authority and activity receive their justification and limit. Against every totalitarian pretension to derive the good of each and of all from the will of all, of the many or the one, Christian theology insists on the inverse derivation. The authority to command men coercively, to make, promulgate and enforce laws within a community, is granted by God for the primary purpose of protecting his good creation against the violent assault of evil-doers.[14] The goods protected by human government and law extend beyond the lives, bodies, and properties of legal individuals to encompass the common spiritual and material goods of public truth, morality, beauty, and the natural environment. To the extent that political rule operates in disregard or defiance of the created natures, ends, and proper relationships of human and non-human creatures, it is unjust and unjustified, whatever the purely human grounds of its legitimacy.[15] Recognition of created order is indispensable to government's observance of the limits of its jurisdiction: exceeding these limits is invariably connected with attack on created goods. For instance, government that outlaws the institution of marriage or interferes with the familial structure of rights and obligations exceeds its jurisdiction as much as government that infringes the individual's freedom of conscience, speech, or lawful possession. For the divinely established structures of communal life — of marriage, family, work, natural justice — are ontologically and morally prior to political right, and circumscribe it, as does the transpolitical vocation of each individual to love God and neighbour as Christ has commanded.[16] In contrast to modern contractual and utilitarian accounts of political right, Christian theology cannot emphasize enough its preservational purpose within God's providential sustaining of the objective order of created goods under the conditions of human sin.

This, then, is the theological articulation of the world that, in our judgement, best unfolds the "apprehension" of the whole as a unity of law and love affirmed by Grant in his essay "In Defence of North America." Grant himself does not, after *Philosophy in the Mass Age*, offer a developed articulation of the world in terms of law and teleology. Indeed, his repeated passing criticisms of Christian Aristotelianism (which, let us note, are implied criticisms of French Catholicism) suggest his overall discontent with natural law theology.[17] His subsequent appeal to Hooker against Lockean liberalism is not especially reassuring, in view of Hooker's abandonment of a teleological account of non-human nature for the greater exaltation of the Law of Reason in human affairs.[18] All his later reflections on law and love in nature appear to be cast in the mould of Simone Weil's Christian gnosticism, which envisages a stringently non-teleological unity of law and love on the natural and supernatural planes.[19] Grant shares Weil's abhorrence of the triumphalist use of natural teleology by the Church to suppress the contradictions of nature and the tragedy of human suffering in the interest of consolidating its structure of worldly authority, and he is similarly sympathetic to her repudiation of all teleological vindications of natural and historical events. In his late article, "Faith and the Multiversity," he once again disowns the "unwise" use of Aristotelian teleology "by official Christianity" with the sharp rebuke that: "The more representable the purpose of the whole was said to be, the more this natural theology became a trivializing, a blasphemy against the cross."[20] These words echo every previous invocation in his writings of the cosmic cross of Weil's mystical theology, the abyss separating necessity and goodness bridged only by the self-emptying love of God.[21] Grant is persuaded by Weil's determined adherence to the "void" of suffering at the heart of faith working through love, at the heart of active consent to the goodness of the world.

He is equally persuaded, however, of the intrinsic relatedness of goodness and purpose, and so calls upon an aesthetic representation of purpose undoubtedly inspired by Weil's interpretation of Plato's *Timaeus*.[22] Drawing on the analogy of the work of art, dear to both Plato and Weil, he portrays the purposiveness of the world as both immanent in the assemblage of "artistic means" (and hence, representable), and transcending those means (hence, unrepresentable).[23] He emphasises the primacy of "intellectual intuition" in our knowledge of the purposiveness, or unity, of the artistic whole; but he does not elaborate the form (or forms) that understanding of the "means" and their interconnectedness should take. Nowhere does he expressly defend a comprehensive teleological understanding of the "means" of God's creation (of human and non-human individuals, relationships and totalities), but confines himself to occasional appeals to traditional teleological perceptions — such as, for instance, the perception that "The love of the beauty of the world in sexual life... [has] some relation to the love of the beauty of the world found in progeny."[24] So when he passes from love of the beauty of the world to the practice of justice towards individual beings, his words about rendering what is due, not only to humans, but "to cattle and bears, wheat and stones," ring somewhat hollow. For to act justly toward any being requires at least implicit knowledge of its purpose and proper action, knowledge of a kind that is susceptible of quite precise conceptual representation. In view of the complex practicalities of just action, Grant's aesthetic account of purposiveness, valid as it may be within its terms, is nevertheless limited and inadequate, and requires completion by means of the conceptual apparatus of theological natural law.

This having been said, we must attend with the utmost seriousness to Grant and Weil's devotion to the centrality of the cross of Christ in thought about the whole. For Christian theology, the Son of God Eternal — Incarnate, Crucified and Resurrected — is the *Alpha* and *Omega*, archetype and end, of created being, and the key to all knowledge of love and law in the world. Human access to created order, goodness, and beauty is not only diminished by sinful blindness, but redirected by the transformation of creation effected in and through the cross and resurrection of Jesus Christ. We must, therefore, pay some attention, albeit insufficient, to the subject of love and law in the renewed creation.

Love and Law in the New Creation

In this theological sphere, too, Grant's thought is an edifice of judgement and correction, relentlessly and meticulously exposing the prevailing intellectual structure of sin among us. He reveals our idolatrous theological tendencies, not only to deny the supra-technological reality of created order, but also to deny the supra-technological reality of Christ's redemption and sanctification of the world. We have absorbed the meaning of both created being and saving being into the technological possibilities of matter for us. Their meaning resides in the unrestrained gratification of our passions and the fantasy of securing of our lives against, on the one hand, the wickedness and frailty of sinful human nature, and on the other, the perceived indifference to human ends of non-human nature. Such immediately attractive theological notions as God's evolution, God's futurity, man's co-creatorship with God, history as liberation, eschatology as open-ended future, all contribute to a blurring of the essential theological distinctions between God's good creation, our fallen creation, and the creation renewed in Christ, as well as of the essential theological relationship of created order to its eschatological fulfillment. They foster the temptation, endemic to our sinful reason, to confuse the transient and ambiguous structures of our present collective thought and action with either the permanent and sufficient structures of created being, or the eschatological structures of redeemed and sanctified being.

In the modern era, liberal and conservative political theologies have both succumbed to the temptation to construe the deficient structures and principles of merely human political reasoning as the laws of nature or of grace. If Locke construed the prudential calculations of many self-seeking political individuals as the authoritative natural basis of civil law and jurisdiction, Hooker construed the prudential calculations of one political individual — the English Queen in Parliament — as the authoritative basis of "outward" ecclesiastical law and jurisdiction. The conservative Hooker shared with the liberal Locke an inflated trust in the capacity of man's unassisted reason to establish the structures of political community — whether commonwealth or Church. Neither gave due weight to the independent authority of scriptural revelation to open up to man's repentant reason God's law in creation and redemption. Hooker's tendency was to view the revelation of communal law in Scripture as God's clarifying confirmation of man's natural political rationality. It is not surprising, then, that he upheld the unitary structure of rule in Church and commonwealth, vehemently opposing Presbyterian and Separatist demands for an autonomous ecclesiastical order that embodied more exactly the Church's divine commission. The much celebrated theological moderation of Richard Hooker, his image as the incarnation of conservative reasonableness, hides from us the encroachment of human law on divine law in his thought.

If Grant's criticism of liberal technological hubris makes any theological impression on thoughtful Christians, it must surely set before them the claim of Christ's law in its power and immediacy. For his criticism is inseparable from his appeal to the authority of the Gospels as surpassing the authority of either of the founding conservatisms of Canada's nationhood. His "negative theology" (to use Grant's self-descriptive phrase), as well as his positive moral arguments — formulated, we should note, in fruitful partnership with his wife Sheila — summon Christians, individually and communally, to embrace the stringency of Christ's law of faith, hope and love, in joyful obedience to his commandments. The fellowship of Christ is summoned to profess God's love in creation and redemption by living according to His revealed ordinances for created nature, and after Christ's human pattern of supernatural love. In disclosing the systemic and pervasive character of our idolatrous freedom, Grant discloses the real scope of the challenge to Christian belief and action in the present. It is no less than holding fast to God's law of love amidst the seductive lawlessness and lovelessness of the world, manifest in the staggering moral facts of mass abortion, human reproductive technologies, nuclear armaments, global economic injustice and ecological destruction. In resisting the temptation to place ourselves above nature in order to dispose of it, Christians must resist the other paramount temptation (upon which resistance everything hangs): that of placing ourselves with nature in order to dispose of Christ. It is to this temptation, as Grant rightly discerns, that traditional natural law theology has too often succumbed. For as all creatures are in and through and to Christ, only so can we know and love them truly. And although this mystery of "the whole" is easier to grasp in the case of man than in the case of the maple tree, it is no more dispensable in the one than in the other.

NOTES

1. George Grant, *Lament for a Nation — The Defeat of Canadian Nationalism*. (Ottawa: Carleton University Press, 1989), pp. 29, 71.

2. Ibid., p. xi.

3. Ibid.

4. Ibid., p. 79.

5. Grant, "Canadian Fate and Imperialism," *Technology and Empire — Perspectives on North America*. (Toronto: House of Anansi Press Limited, 1969), p. 68.

6. Grant, *Philosophy in the Mass Age*. (Toronto: Copp Clark Publishing, 1959), p. 100.

7. Ibid., p. 99.

8. Grant, "In Defence of North America," p. 35.

9. Grant, "Faith and the Multiversity," *Technology and Justice*. (Toronto: House of Anansi Press Limited, 1986), p. 38.

10. My explication of natural kinds and *tele* is greatly indebted to the writings of Etienne Gilson, especially *The Philosophy of St. Thomas Aquinas* (tr. Edward Bullough, ed. G.A. Elrington; Cambridge, 1929) and *The Spirit of Mediaeval Philosophy* (tr. A.H.C. Downes; New York, 1936). I refer the sceptical scientists who object to the concepts of natural kinds and ends to his masterful replies. Another useful defence of the philosophical concept of "nature" against scientific phenomenalism is found in Jacques Maritain's *The Degrees of Knowledge*. I am also indebted to the theology of created order in Oliver O'Donovan's *Resurrection and Moral Order* (Leicester/Grand Rapids, 1986).

11. That "probability" in quantum theory is meaningful only as necessity is argued by Simone Weil in her paper "Reflections on Quantum Theory": "...the consequences of quantum theory, which derived from the study of probability, led [scientists] to introduce probability among the atoms themselves. Thus the trajectories of atomic particles are no longer called necessary but probable, and there is no necessity anywhere. And yet, probability can only be defined as a rigorous necessity, of whose conditions some are known and others unknown; the conception of probability, divorced from that of necessity, is meaningless." On *Science, Necessity and the Love of God*. (Oxford, 1968), p. 61.

12   In the Biblical portrayal of man's alienated condition, his work is toilsome, beset by pain, uncertainty, and futility. ("And to Adam he said: '... cursed is the ground because of you; in toil you shall eat of it all the days of your life; thorns and thistles it shall bring forth to you .... In the sweat of your face you shall eat bread till you return to the ground....'"; *Genesis* 3: 17-19.) His dependence on nature's sustenance is ridden with anxiety and humiliation and pervaded by the consciousness of his own mortality in the face of nature's vast endurance. ("What does man gain by all the toil at which he toils under the sun? A generation goes, and a generation comes, but the earth remains forever," says the Preacher of the Book of *Ecclesiastes* 1:3-4, voicing the sentiment of the Biblical "wisdom tradition.") His striving is perpetually frustrated by an insatiable craving and ambition that is an unrelenting goad to toil. ("... the eye is not satisfied with seeing, nor the ear filled with hearing." *Ecclesiastes* 1:8.)

13   It is entirely mistaken to understand Christ's law as commanding a reciprocity of virtuous conduct based on self-interested calculation, as if it read: "Do good to others in order that you may receive good from them." Rather, the phrase "whatever you wish that men would do to you" intends the ethical content and not the motive of the law, and is an epistemological guide to it. Thus, the commandment may be paraphrased: "The good that you owe to others is the good that you wish to receive."

14   The chief Biblical locus for the theological justification of coercive public authority has always been Roma*ns* 13:1-7. Here, St. Paul exhorts the Roman Christians to be "subject to the governing authorities," inasmuch as government is "instituted by God" (v. 1) and rulers are the "servant[s] of God to execute his wrath on the wrongdoer" (v. 4), so that "he who resists ... what God has appointed... will incur judgement" (v. 2). However, they are to "be subject not only to avoid God's wrath, but also for the sake of conscience" (v. 5). The wrongdoer violates God's law, not merely man's law; and God's law is associated throughout the Bible with the protection of created goods. A set of Old Testament passages considered important for political theology concerns the authority divinely invested in the human comnunity to avenge with the penalty of death the crime of wilfully destroying the fundamental created good of human life: see, for example, *Genesis* 9:6; *Deuteronomy* 19:13.

15   This is not to deny any authority to political rule that acts against created nature, but to deny it the authority of acting justly. Christian political thought has long admitted that even unjust rule serves the common good by averting the greater evil of civil anarchy. Nevertheless, it is essential to dispute the exaggerated emphasis placed by modern liber-

alism on procedural legitimacy by modern liberalism in establishing political authority. Duly elected government, while possessing the authority conferred by popular consent, may still not possess the authority conferred by rendering substantive justice.

16   This is the leading argument of Emile Brunner's much neglected book, *Justice and the Social Order* (tr. Mary Hottinger; London, 1945) which ranks among the few theologically weighty Protestant accounts of politics written in this century.

17   This discontent is implied in Grant's early criticism of the tendency of "rational theology" to trivialize the fact of evil and the meaning of Christ's crucifixion, by basing its account of human freedom on an undialectical identification of necessity and goodness ("Two Theological Languages", 1947). In *Philosophy in the Mass Age* (1959) Grant expressly criticises the traditional natural law theory of Roman Catholicism for lacking insight into the infinite transcendence of human freedom over natural objects, an insight belonging to Enlightenment and Reformation consciousness (pp. 6, 12, 28, 49-50). His concluding outline for the synthesis of law and freedom in an "absolute morality" does not attempt to rehabilitate natural theology. In his essay "In Defence of North America" (1968), he returns to his original theological objection to natural teleology: namely, its deflection of men's attention from "the surd mystery of evil" and from "the only true illumination of that mystery, the crucifixion apprehended in faith as the divine humiliation." (*Technology and Empire*, p. 20). Significantly, in *Lament For A Nation*, he refrains from theological criticism of French Catholicism, as ill-suiting the thrust of his historical-political argument.

18   Departing from St. Thomas, Hooker, in Book 1 of *The Laws of Ecclesiastical Polity*, sharply distinguishes Nature's Law from the Law of Reason, arguing that those sub-human creatures subject to Nature's Law are moved by God only as the efficient cause of their motion, whereas beings subject to the Law of Reason are moved by Him as the final cause of their motion. *The Works of Richard Hooker* (7th edition, ed. John Keble; New York, 1970), Vol. I, pp. 210-12.

19   Weil's most instructive writings for understanding her Christian gnosticism are collected in *Intimations of Christianity Among The Ancient Greeks*, a volume of essays taken partly from *La Source Grecque* and from *Les Intuitions Pre-chretiennes* (ed. and tr. E.C. Geissbuhler; Boston, 1958).

20   Grant, "Faith and the Multiversity," *Technology and Justice*, p. 44.

21   While Weil's cosmic crucifixion theology is the backdrop to all Grant's reflections on the distance separating necessity and goodness, it is explicitly addressed in his poignant encounter with the thought of Dostoevsky, in "Fyodor Dostoevsky" (*Architects of Modern Thought*, Toronto, 1959, pp. 71-83).

22   This encroachment is especially apparent in Hooker's discussion of the complex interaction of divine and human law in the institution of episcopacy — its apostolic origin and continuing authority — in *Ecclesiastical Polity*, Book 7.

23   Grant, "Faith and the Multiversity," *Technology and Justice*, p. 46.

24   Ibid., p. 52.

GRANT, NATURAL LAW AND SIMONE WEIL

John Kirby and Louis Greenspan

O'Donovan's panel responded to her carefully constructed argument for the recovery of the natural law tradition respectfully, but with scepticism. Basing her paper on the evocation of this tradition in Grant's writings, O'Donovan urged that Grant's project be clarified, purged of inconsistencies and be brought to completion with a systematic doctrine of natural law. Panelists agreed with her that Grant's teachings on natural law seem paradoxical; it was observed that, while Grant saw natural law as the inescapable alternative to a modernity adrift without spiritual or moral grounding, he was reluctant to draw on the natural law tradition as a source of specific ethical and political judgements. However, most of the panellists believed that the theological tradition of natural law required a cautious approach. Even those who upheld its continuing validity thought of natural law as being visible through a glass, darkly. Fuller, for example, endorsed O'Donovan's account of modernity as "caught between conservatism as unreflective traditionalism and liberalism as unreflective innovation," but he questioned whether the invocation of a beautiful expression of the cosmic whole could necessarily "absolve us from the sticky difficulties of practical life."

Despite this general consensus on O'Donovan's paper, there was little consensus among panellists on an interpretation of Grant's writing or on his critique of natural law. Two interpretive problems in particular came to the fore: could natural law provide a detailed structure of political ethics, as O'Donovan seemed to suggest; and how could one assess the influence on Grant of Simone Weil, whom O'Donovan saw as the nemesis of the natural law tradition.

The participants fell roughly into two groups: those who thought that the natural law tradition could not provide a basis for ethics or politics in the modern world (adherents to this view included

John Dourley, Louis Greenspan and Randall Marlin), and those who held that the natural law was still a relevant issue but hesitated to tie it down to a specific content. This position was shared by John Robertson, Tim Fuller and John Kirby. Greenspan's view was that, no matter how compelling or promising the natural law tradition might have been both in general and to Grant, there is no bridge between it and the real world of modernity. Sartre's complaint that Marxism was right about everything in general and about nothing in particular could apply equally to natural law. Thus, while Grant the philosopher stressed natural law, Grant the activist seemed to ignore it. Earlier in the conference, Dennis Lee spoke of the emptiness of modernity reducing all moral and political thought to silence. Again, Greenspan noted that Grant the philosopher may have lamented this emptiness but Grant the activist still managed to fire off quite a few loud and well-aimed salvos.

Greenspan maintained that Grant the activist used one of the modern discourses, that of liberalism, very effectively. Many of his positions such as his anti-imperialism, and even his rejection of the right to abortion were couched in terms that would have been familiar to Kant and John Stuart Mill. O'Donovan called for an ethic of environmentalism, of care for non-human nature. She claimed that such care comes easily to the discourse of natural law with its regard for *telos*. Greenspan noted that the existing environmental movement usually looks to more contemporary discourse — once again, to liberalism and its call for the rights of sentient beings.

With respect to O'Donovan's objection to Grant's sympathy for Simone Weil, Greenspan noted the strength of Weil's influence on Grant, characterizing it as a Christianity of subversion placed like a bomb into the framework of a Christianity of rational structure. But, as Greenspan remarked, Grant made no comprehensive statement on Weil, and the exact nature of her influence on him is difficult to discern.

Marlin speculated about how Jacques Ellul, who also influenced Grant, might have viewed our discussion. Basing himself on Ellul's *The Theological Foundation of Law*, he suggested that Ellul would have agreed with O'Donovan's critique of modernity, but would have insisted on another remedy.

Ellul called for a political order rooted in Scripture rather than in natural law. Scripture called for a society based on compassion, justice, protection of the weak and the well-being of the miserable. These, Marlin said, are the foundations of a political order based on revelation; he emphasized that "in this sense revelation is authoritative, that it is state law's adherence to divine law that makes it acceptable to its subjects."

But whereas the natural law tradition emphasized a political rule based on reason, rule by revelation could mean an authoritarian rule by the few who had received the divine word. Conscious of this consequence, Marlin denied that Ellul's call for a return to Scripture implied a return to the mediaeval domination of society by the Church. In Ellul's conception the Church is a conscience that prods, rather than an authority that rules. The Church reminds the state that law must be grounded in divine authority, and that social cohesion must not be based on force alone. Accordingly, the Church could be involved in politics and in the secular life of society but it would not be motivated to pursue its political interests. Marlin concluded that Ellul, O'Donovan and Grant have recognized the emptiness of modern theories of contractualism and utilitarianism. They seek the true bonds of society and thus they give us a common source of inspiration.

Dourley focused on Grant's interest in how modern man might express his relationship to the divine in a world that no longer employed the language of Thomistic-Aristotelian Christianity. He saw a parallel in Tillich's conception of God as ground of being, as depth of reason. In this context, Dourley wondered if Grant's sympathy for gnosticism grew out of a "radical sense of divine immanence" like that of Jacob Boehme or Hegel, who held that God created man to assist Him in articulating a fundamental self-contradiction that could only be resolved with the co-operation of man. Such a view, Dourley suggested, could contribute to the renewal and broadening of contemporary Christian thinking about man and society.

Thus, panelists who discounted the continued relevance of natural law were divided among those who believed that modern ethics and politics could proceed on the basis of secular ideas of modernity, and those who believed that they needed firmer roots in theological concepts other than natural law. Other panelists, however cautious about natural law, were unwilling to dismiss it.

John Robertson began by agreeing with O'Donovan that a firm doctrine of natural law was required to ground both the intrinsic, as opposed to the instrumental, worth of created things as well as the moral foundation of positive law. Like O'Donovan, he associated such a doctrine with a biblical conception of creation.

Following Gadamer, Robertson urged caution on those claiming to know the content of natural law which functions best as a "limiting concept" or "regulative ideal" to use Kant's terms, to only be invoked from time to time as a critique of positive law. In classical Christian natural law teaching, revelation clarified, confirmed and supplemented the discoveries of reason. Now, for Grant, Christ was the decisive, but not the exclusive source of revelation, which could occur in certain other areas of human experience. Indeed, Grant's understanding of the role of revelation benefited, said Robertson, from the influence of Simone Weil's appreciation of beauty as an intimation of the divine beyond human willing. He found in her writing an account of a kind of revelation in the general sacramentality of the universe, which included the aesthetic experience.

At the same time, Robertson objected to the influence on Grant of Weil's "extreme other-worldliness and asceticism," which seemed to contradict traditional doctrines of creation. He preferred the earlier Grant, who found in Hegel a reconciliation of the divine and the human, the eternal and the temporal in which "the world is really confirmed and hallowed rather than negated ... the real meaning of 'sublation' or *aufhebung*."

Fuller referred to the natural law tradition with sympathy, but recognized its internal problems as well as the difficulty of using it to address the problems of modernity. He didn't reject natural law as the basis of a critique of modernity, but he questioned the possibility of regarding it as authoritative.

Referring to the critique of natural law from within the tradition itself, Fuller noted that it is not at all clear that the natural law is a "theological" tradition. For Thomas and others, natural law is available to all enquirers "whether they have the benefit of revelation or not." But a Christian could not accept natural law grounded in reason alone as a court of appeal in the ethical problems of life. To illustrate, according to Aquinas the laws governing private property, or establishing the rights of private property, did not flow directly from natural law; rather, they were added of necessity, and by human ingenuity, to the human order. While it is of ultimate importance to Aquinas, and while it forms his understanding of the purpose of the law, it is not from the Christian framework that he derives his definition of the law.

Christianity teaches that, after the fall, there is a clash between the law of nature and the law of love, a clash that is manifested in many ways. One of the most important manifestations, Fuller recalled, was the clash between the individual and the social. The "adjustment of the individual and the social must go on continually in human life." And these are matters for practical reason, matters which must continually be reworked. In opposition to O'Donovan, Fuller suggested that reconciling the law of love with the rule of law is a vision which leaves unresolved the practical questions as we experience them in our daily lives.

Turning to the possibility of basing a contemporary ethos on natural law, Fuller examined O'Donovan's proposal to use the tradition as the basis of an environmentalist ethos, in that the '*telos* of a natural substance is a constraint upon human action'. But, Fuller asks, since O'Donovan admits that nature is for human use and that destruction of natural objects is sometimes legitimate, "who will adjudicate claims of human use against the claims of natural things?" Presumably it will have to be human beings, which puts us in the central role we are trying to disclaim. Thus, Fuller argues, "the law of love actually requires us to go beyond what the natural law teaches us, even if it does not contradict the natural law. The vision that Dr.O'Donovan lovingly expressed cannot be legislated."

"What can be authoritative?" was Fuller's persistent theme. He pointed out that the task of choosing between a "natural versus a scientific understanding of the world," is one of the novelties of the modern situation. But on what basis can we make such a choice? If we choose the natural, we tie Christianity to a particular, prescientific world. By what authority do we do so?

Fuller, then, has taken seriously O'Donovan's contention that modernity cannot stand on its own feet, hence the return of natural law to the agenda, but he asks by what criteria we can choose between them and who will choose. Moreover, how can the language of Thomistic-Aristotelian Christianity find any resonance in the modern soul, a soul which has in the emptiness of modernity been reduced to silence? Our problem is not the lack of a theological concept of natural law, but the absence of a unifying culture whose terms find expression through an authoritative voice. Fuller's point is that the loss of cultural agreement concerning natural law theology occurred not so much because we desired that loss, but because it came to be viewed by many as unavoidable.

Kirby endorsed Fuller's views on natural law, particularly his discussion of its intrinsic complexity and the problems it raises in connection with the question of authority and modernity. Kirby observed that the discussion of Grant and natural law had raised questions about the unity of Grant's thought. Thus, unity seemed threatened both by the multiplicity of political and philosophical positions Grant had taken at various times and by the theological adequacy of what appeared to be his fundamental convictions. Grant's views on Canadian nationhood, technology, the concept of history, and abortion had in fact been associated with many different schools of thought. And his religious views could, in Louis Greenspan's view, be understood variously as those of a Churchman and those of a subversive.

But within this diversity, Kirby argued, one had to recognize such crucial indications as Grant's regular invocation of Platonic conceptions of virtue, and the later, clear rejections of Hegel and existentialism. And if he never again wrote about natural law with the eloquence and simplicity of *Philosophy in the Mass Age*, neither did he ever repudiate that account of human excellence.

Rather, the questions about justice Grant so pointedly raised in all his later works appeared, to Kirby, as a sustained meditation on natural law, an attempt by means of the *via negativa* to determine what the love of the good might mean in a disordered age. "What are we fitted for? What are we claimed by? Is there a law we discover beyond our making? What is due to our fellow man, to cattle, to forests, to polar bears? Is there today any unqualified meaning of 'ought'?"

The unity of Grant's questions about the love of the good was matched, Kirby suggested, by the constancy of his devotion to Simone Weil, whom he regarded as a "genius" and a "saint." In her astringent reflections on necessity, justice and love, Grant seemed to find an illumination of the imperatives of both Plato and the Gospel, to which he returned, in the words of another writer, as to the teaching of "a modern Diotima."

Natural law, it was agreed, was a looming presence in Grant's writings rather than a doctrine. It coexisted with other presences that sometimes seemed contradictory. The panelists presented a spectrum of possible positions on Grant; but they shared an uneasiness about translating into doctrine the presence of natural law in his thought.

GRANT'S TECHNOLOGY AND JUSTICE:
BETWEEN PHILOSOPHY AND PROPHECY

Kenneth Minogue

I met George Grant only once, in 1979, on what was, I think, his sixty-first birthday. It was with Bill Christian and Julie Beatty, who sat in the back of the car icing a birthday cake. There was a seminar which made clear what a born teacher Grant was. At the end of it I think I said that he had turned Plato into an Anglican and he expressed surprise that I should find this an odd idea. Grant was a philosopher, and the way to keep a philosopher's ideas alive is by rethinking and testing them. Such is my aim.

Philosophers these days come in all shapes and sizes and their dissensions are such that one philosopher may not recognize another as even belonging to the same species. Grant didn't think much of analytic philosophers, those who dominated the profession in the North America of his time. He was bewitched by Nietzsche and fascinated by Heidegger, but his philosophical centre of gravity was Plato and the Greeks. Because he took them to have thought through the question of justice, he believed it his educational duty to make this philosophy come alive for his students. This was far more important than going down in the history of philosophy with a footnote detailing some minor technical achievement — Grant's fork, or Grantian ethics. In any case, Grant was almost too involved in his own time to be a pure philosopher. His was a complex achievement — philosophy, prophecy, political argument, and social criticism. It is all there. It is indeed all there in the very title *Technology and Justice* of the book which primarily concerns me. For what Grant really means, of course, is Technology *versus* Justice.

Grant's procedure, here as elsewhere, is to analyse an apparently harmless remark by way of context or implication, so that it becomes revelatory of the hidden presuppositions of what he seeks to understand — in this case, and usually, the character of the modern world. The luckless utterer of the remark in *Technology and Justice* was a computer scientist, who said: "The computer does not impose on us the ways it should be used."[1] Grant observes that this remark takes the computer to be a neutral instrument; what it expresses is the dominant liberal view that we "have certain technological capacities; it is up to us to use those capacities for decent human purposes."[2]

Grant's first move in drawing out the significance of the remark might be designed to develop the antinomy of the inside and the outside. The scientist thinks he is "outside" the computer and is free to determine how it is employed; but his mistake is to see the computer in abstraction from the whole cast of mind which produced it. Both he and the computer are part of "technology," and hence the idea that the computer does not impose itself on us misleads us as to our true situation:

> Common sense may tell us that the computer is an instrument, but it is an instrument from within the destiny which *does* 'impose' itself upon us, and there-fore the computer *does* impose.[3]

There is a certain imprecision here which seems to me a common feature of Grant's work, and, while not fatal to his general project, it deserves attention as a kind of "slippage." All that this sentence asserts is that there is a "destiny" which imposes itself upon us and that the computer is part of that destiny. The destiny is the imposer; we and the computer would seem to be its consequences. Hence it is not strictly true that the *computer* imposes itself. This is, of course, a tiny point, but it is the kind of thing I find a little unsettling in Grant's argument and it illustrates how very thoroughly he took the high-minded philosophical path to the exclusion of underlabouring concern with the purely technical features of argument.[4]

The wider difficulty, however, is that if the question is to be treated dialectically so that all the connections are brought into focus as an explanation of the totality of our situation, then the distinction between "us" and "our destiny" will have to be overcome. It is indeed true — it could hardly be otherwise — that the way the computer is used will depend on the mental universe of those who invented and use it. At this point, the argument gets its force from the identity, "we are what we are." But Grant's argument has, simultaneously, another side to it: we are not what we are, because we, or at least the philosopher Grant, can stand back and criticize the modern world from a standpoint independent of what are supposed to be the presuppositions of the whole society. Philosophy is thus an Archimedean point which is outside the philosopher's own society and which may even, perhaps, supply an external prophetic impetus to change social direction.

How the antinomy works depends at this point on how one draws the line between the grand inclusive abstractions (society, modernity) on the one hand, and philosophy on the other. If we remove philosophy, then society will inevitably look rather mindless, driven, and mechanical. If, however, we take philosophy to be one social activity among others in any given civilization, then we destroy the bold critical remarks about the narrowness of its presuppositions. Further, Grant understands this civilizational thing outside of which he locates himself in a manner that was very fashionable in earlier decades: as a "system."

> Every instrument of mass culture is a pressure alienating the individual from himself as a free being.... the individual becomes (whether on the assembly line, in the office, or in the department store) an object to be administered by scientific efficiency experts.... Modern culture, through the movies, newspapers and television, through commercialized recreation and popular advertising, forces the individual into the service of the capitalist system around him.[5]

There is quite a lot in this vein, familiar to us from the enthusiasms of the sixties, and every sentence, of course, induces in the reader a countervailing resistance to precisely what is being described as inescapable. Like all followers of Plato, Grant is drawn inexorably to invoke a distinction between the philosopher and the passion-driven majority of mankind, the distinction modern classicists have domesticated as that between elite and mass.

The philosopher thus takes up his stand on a point somewhere outside the city and describes, often with some distaste, what he sees.

But inside-outside is a real antinomy precisely because there is another inside, or rather a variety of insides, ready to swallow up even the philosopher himself. One of them is the passage of time. To read Grant now is to be reminded that he was, in many respects, a man of his time, which was the late 'fifties and 'sixties, a time of intense disillusion, from a variety of standpoints, with the forms of life found in liberal democratic societies. It is understandable that those who shared such an antipathy (Grant from his Anglican point of view, Marxists from out of the depths of their commitment to the Enlightenment) should have plundered the same repertoire of examples and expressions. Grant disliked television, life insurance, teenage dating, and the supermarket, the military-industrial complex, and many of the other familiar targets of the time. Like Heidegger, he hated nihilism and gadgetry and there is no doubt that those of us who care more than most about cultural riches will cheer him to the echo. But we cannot, in my view, cheer him all the way, because the very idea of "mass society" is an ideological fantasy. The Christian in Grant periodically recognized this; the Platonist let it rip. And it is this Platonizing strain which links him to the more familiar Marxist critics of the time. His admiration of Platonic virtue made him dangerously susceptible to the siren call of authenticity in its many modern forms. His standpoint, he claims, is one above the alienations of what he takes to be modern technological society. Many of these, however, are the alienations (if such they be) of the human condition itself.

Grant, then, is a virtuoso exponent of the argument that what seems like an outside purchase is merely a fragment of what it is we are trying to understand. Instruments such as the computer, common sense practicality, as well as the very standards of justice by which we might evaluate how we use machinery, all come "from within the very technology we are attempting to represent" or belong "to the same destiny of modern reason."[6] It is clear that Grant summons us to ascend by exclusions to ever higher and more rarefied points of vantage.

One of the most important of these lower vantage points is the Cartesian tradition of modern philosophy. Grant joins many others in rejecting it.

His argument on the validity of the subject-object distinction is not concerned with the question of whether such a distinction obscures the truth, or makes it categorically unavailable to us. The modern paradigm of knowledge, he tells us, is the project of reason to gain objective knowledge. The world thus turns into an "object," something from which we have separated ourselves, and as an object, it is "summonsed" and forced to justify itself by answering our questions. This is a curiously melodramatic view of the relation between the knower and the known and, again, one is tempted to connect it with the nearly contemporary conception described by Herbert Marcuse, of the violent and interrogatory character of analytical and linguistic philosophers. What is clear, I think, is that Grant is not really concerned here with epistemological questions but is thinking rather, of the relation between Western man and the world of nature which is subjected to practical purposes. Thinking of the drilling and scooping of modern industrial operations, he reflects this element of violence back to the fundamental paradigm of knowledge involved. His objection to technological assumptions (which he calls a "language," implying that those who speak that language cannot utter things which are unsayable in it) is not based on the familiar ground that the subject-object distinction dooms us to scepticism; he objects because these assumptions exclude goodness and beauty:

> ...any statement about the beauty of the world is so easily doubted in our era, because it appears meaningless within the dominant language of modern science.[7]

Similarly, goodness has, as it were, had the *telos* scooped out of it and can now only express preferences. At worst, "goodness" is replaced by "value."

The moral point is given in Grant's remark, "Anything apprehended as resource cannot be apprehended as beautiful."[8] He goes on to regret the day in which Canada has been understood by many people as a vast resource; even its people have been so described.

Now, one way of considering this very point is given by Michael Oakeshott, as he elaborates his view of modes of experience in relation to poetry as a specific mode. Oakeshott quotes the reminiscence of visitors to the Owen Falls in Lake Victoria:

We have spent three hours watching the waters and revolving plans to harness and bridle them. So much power running to waste, such a coign of vantage unoccupied, such a level to control the natural forces of Africa ungripped cannot but vex and stimulate the imagination.[9]

This is, Oakeshott argues, a quite different image from that of Keats:

The moving waters at their priest-like task of pure ablution round earth's human shores.[10]

But in Oakeshott's view, the practical and the poetic modes are both available to us, and there must be few who (whatever the dominance of practice) do not at times entertain a poetic image. Grant, however, wants to identify practice and technology with the modern world, attributing to the elaboration of the implications the very language and repertoire of perceptions available to us in the modern world. Certainly Grant's own life defies this identification by including both kinds of experience. Once more, we discover Grant sitting on his own elevation and gazing at a limited view of the "inside" of the civilisation within which he lived. And that must be explained.

Grant supplies us with a familiar fall-of-man story. Crudely speaking (and I cannot go beyond the crude), the Greek philosophers focused on justice and the nature of being human, questions which are central to the business of leading a properly human life. Christianity is the presentation in another idiom of the same preoccupations. The main conclusion of these meditations is that man is a limited creature and is not free to allow his will to determine what he should do. Somewhere around the twelfth or thirteenth centuries the elements of our modern scientific culture were already emerging and they have been growing stronger ever since. Indeed, so strong have they grown that they are beginning to obliterate even our memory that there was anything else.

This is why the dying out of careful philosophical study in Canada is one factor helping to produce our dead-Grant's work thus seems to belong to the idiom of: Where did we go wrong? Was it with Socrates and Plato? Or Christianity? Protestantism? The Enlighten-

ment? Everyone will be familiar with famous exemplars of this genre.[11]

Let me, however, juxtapose against this what seems to me to be
the crucial sequence of events, and their implications. The Greeks
construed nature as a kind of living whole animated by a principle of
reason which allowed Man (as represented by those few possessing
real rational capacity) to align himself with the principles of the
universe. Such alignment was the key to harmony, both inner and
external, and it required understanding of the ideal world and some
knowledge of the place of the disorderly passions. The Greeks thus
believed that there was a natural order of things and that human beings
had a built-in tendency to diverge from that order. "Reason" was
recognising and sustaining that order, "passion" stood for propensi-
ties to diverge. Now, if the matter is put abstractly in this way, it will
be found to cover pretty well all the common beliefs held by other
civilizations, and indeed by all sophisticated people up until the
beginning of the Middle Ages. This sketch can easily be modified to
incorporate the creator and the fall of man, which causes us to make
abstract and fragmentary worlds out of our self-consciousness, and,
mistaking these for reality itself, to fall into the sin of pride. Here, then,
is a view of nature and reason that would seem to unite the philosophers of the ancient world and, in the early day of Christianity, their
mortal enemies, the Christians.

What, then, is the change that leads on to the modern world?
Let us leave aside the most vital arguments, which are theological, and
focus on the doctrine that we can only understand what we have made
ourselves. This was taken to mean that we could understand society,
language and mathematics, but that nature, since it was created by
God, would be forever alien to us. Unable to penetrate directly into the
secrets of nature by reason (as the Greeks imagined themselves to do)
moderns perforce had recourse to mathematical models and the experimental method. As their confidence grew, they put increasing
emphasis on the Biblical proposition that the earth and all its fruits
were given to man to use according to his convenience, a doctrine
elaborated notably by Francis Bacon, and fully alive in the nationalists
of the seventeenth century. It was in expounding the assumptions of
this modern view of reason and nature that the dualism of subject and
object came to haunt modern philosophy.

It seems to me fairly clear that Grant's affirmation of mythic consciousness and his espousal of Plato expresses a yearning to return to a world in which man will find his place in nature; hence the terrifying adventure of modernity, in which everything seems to be permitted, will again be recognised as dangerous pride. It is an understandable judgement and aligns him with the political Greens who also want to draw back from the rapacious ingenuity of modern man. It even aligns him with his old enemy, Bertrand Russell, who in his last years began to discover the value of a kind of environmental *pietas*.

The crux of the matter comes when Grant discusses euthanasia and abortion. Here are two cases in which man has taken his destiny into his own hands, and Grant appears before us as a prophet warning of the horrible consequences of making technological ingenuity and human convenience the test of how we conduct our life. Let me elucidate and comment upon what I take to be some crucial stages of the argument.

The modern world is essentially technological, and Grant wishes to play down any distinction between science and technology, that is, between trying to understand the world in terms of general laws and manipulating it according to our desires. It is by refusing to make this distinction that he is able to succeed in identifying objectivity with manipulability. The attempt to see something as it actually is, independent of any response to it on our part is, in Grant's view, indistinguishable from treating the object from a practical point of view as being, at least incipiently, a thing to be subjected to our purposes. In my view, this is simply an error about human possibility, but I think I can see why Grant wants to insist on it. Technology and science in the modern sense first became self-conscious at the beginning of the seventeenth century and they have been historically entirely intertwined. This constitutes what we might call Grant's Fall, the moment at which the will to power kicked aside all the essential props of justice and embarked upon what he rather hopefully describes as the "experiment" of modernity. Justice, therefore, was merely a vestige surviving in the interstices of European life, its source in sound philosophy having been blocked. Most of those involved in this experiment did not really understand what they were doing. Grant follows many others (Strauss, for example) in thinking that the one figure who did see right through all this was Nietzsche. He it was who recognised that the modern project must involve discarding human lives that did not measure up to some shifting standards described in phrases such as "quality of life": As Grant interprets Nietzsche:

> The human creating of quality of life beyond the little perspectives of good and evil by a building, rejecting, annihilating way of thought is the statement that politics is the technology of making the human race greater than it has yet been.[12]

As is often the case with Grant, one can sympathize with the larger vision more easily than with the detail: Nietzsche was not concerned with politics and he certainly did not think that a human race made greater would be the result of a kind of *technology*.

All of these portentous consequences are made to ride on the epistemological distinction between subject and object. Objectivity is the parent of exploitative rapacity. Yet it cannot fail to strike the reader that Greek and Roman rapacity in the use of slaves for mining and other enterprises had very little to learn from the corrupting doctrines to be found in Genesis 2 and Francis Bacon. And if such a thought does strike the reader, he is likely to move one stage further and observe that Grant seems to assume that the conduct of practical men is a kind of practical conclusion drawn from the premises of philosophers. Grant is aware, of course, that the relationship can be reversed. In his radical vein he is highly critical of the role of private corporations in turning universities into suppliers of useful objective facts for capitalist manipulation of the world. But then, these corporations themselves are thought ultimately to emerge from the collapse of a philosophical understanding of justice around the beginning of the modern era.

Abortion and euthanasia are seen as among the long-term fruits of the modern experiment. The presuppositions and the practical world come together in such judgements as the following:

> A technological vision of man or woman as an object means that we can apply our 'improvements' to them as objects with increasing efficiency. Once we deny justice to any human life, then we are well on the road

> to the kind of thinking that impels a fascist dictatorship
> to the horrors of the death camp and the purge.[13]

In this passage, the running together of the scientific and practical understandings of the world is achieved by asserting that the one "means" the other. We find ourselves here at one of those familiar Grantian junctions of philosophy, politics, ethics, and prophecy. Grant affirms the Christian doctrine that we ought to love other human beings as our neighbours, as ourselves, and in the present argument he is concerned to head off any attempt to set any fancy limits to what constitutes a human being. He has discovered one appalling lunatic who wants to define personhood in terms of the IQ level. Modern developments are leading towards the exclusion from the class of humanity of the foetus, the feeble-minded, the aged and disabled, no doubt the brain-dead; and in an ecstasy of the "slippery slope" argument) Grant adds that the "less economically privileged" might soon be added to the list. But then, in the passage quoted, the rigour slips, and we get a bit of political cliche. The "dictatorship" must be "fascist" for effect, and death camps and purges are not to the point. They don't have anything to do with the medico-ethical issues he is concerned with. In any case, Machiavelli, back in the sixteenth century, had nothing to learn about the purge; nor, for that matter did the Roman masters of the proscription list, nor the Athenians as they dealt with the Melians.

Grant's real theme is the collapse of limits, and the real realm in which he operates is not what cannot be done, because horrible things have always been done, but what cannot be thought. The "death of God" might mean that "All is permitted," but it is a permission for which earlier generations didn't bother to wait. Without in any way doubting Grant's central point that the current intellectual situation may be the source of a unique danger, one must be clear that there is much plausibility in the view that the statistical horror of the twentieth century is purely a matter of technology in the most obvious sense. Ancient wars were often genocidal, and being in the path of the Golden Horde was in no way preferable to succumbing to the Panzers.

It is, then, the unique danger stemming from philosophy which must be the central concern of the argument. How has this danger come about? It is here that Grant is at his best. It is the collapse of philosophy in universities that is central to his argument, and this collapse has several aspects. The first stage, we might say, was the abandonment of the Aristotelian synthesis which incorporated a concern with final causes as central to the enterprise of thinking and understanding the world. As a result, moral issues were pushed to the periphery of philosophical interest. In more recent times the dynamic of this process has turned philosophers into logical technicians marooned, as it were, in the meta. And as a further working out of this dynamic, the universities have been invaded by a whole host of new social sciences which study human beings objectively and thus create a civilization based on nothing more substantial than will and persuasion. The convenience of the strong is the only abiding principle and modern experience shows just how ruthless this can be and what horrifying consequences it can generate.

A further aspect is hinted at. In earlier centuries, those who studied philosophy (in the full Greek sense) at universities commonly became clergymen and priests. Moving from the rostrum to the pulpit, they sustained among the entire population a view of life in which a sense of eternal things was present. But now, Grant complains, along with Hegel and Nietzsche, the day that used to begin with morning prayers is early devoted to nothing more substantial than the reading of worldly things in the newspapers. Thus, the evil of the modern world is that the intellectual and institutional supports of the good life have collapsed.

Grant is very good at describing how the case for abortion and euthanasia must still be made by way of euphemism, despite the dominance of technological ideas and the collapse of philosophy; and in warning us of the dangers implicit in such charming ideas as "quality of life" he is performing the critical office of the philosopher. It is also in this context that he makes genuine philosophical moves, as when he argues that those who base the case for abortion on a woman's right to choose — to choose to deny any rights to the foetus — are calling into question the very basis on which one might attribute rights to any human being. Yet here, too, I think that he does not press the argument far enough. He does not wish to explode altogether the notion of rights as being merely a piece of moral dogmatism. He does not wish to do this because he seems to think, possibly opportunistically, that the language of rights is a way of conserving some vestiges of the

Greek idea of the good life. He may also possibly recognise in the idea of rights an offshoot of the Christian conception of a human being.

My own view is that he goes wrong in trying to find Greek foundations for these admirable moral views. This is a mistake for both historical and philosophical reasons. The historical reason is that the Greeks had no particular view of the sanctity of life. They seem to have practised infanticide without any scruple. The philosophical reason is that Greek humanism is in the highest degree qualitative. "Man" is not a creature made by God in his image, but a rational part of nature graded in terms of participation in reason. Women, slaves, metics, barbarians were all in some degree or other imperfectly rational, and, to that extent, imperfectly human. The idea of attaching rights to human beings as such is not something that would have detained Plato for long. He was not, after all, an Anglican.

When one's judgement of a body of work wobbles, the reason is usually that one's criteria are fuzzy. And there is no doubt that in Grant's case the problem arises from his use of "philosophy." It is, for him, a gauntlet thrown down to the Bertrand Russells and the Ludwig Wittgensteins of this world in order to insist that nothing is genuinely philosophical unless it arises from the question: What is the good life for man? In other words, by "philosophy" Grant commonly means "moral judgement in logical depth." Thus he remarks in passing:

> ... to accept the difference between intended action and
> the meaning of event is to have insisted that historical
> explanation only completes itself within philosophy.[14]

Any historian, of course, will see meanings in an event beyond those which were intended by the actor or actors. So, too, will the moralist who condemns as bad an act justified by the actor on prudential grounds. Philosophy need not be involved at all. But if we turn the sentence around, we must recognise that what Grant is after is something called "meaning."

> In a period when meaning has become obscure, or to
> use other language, when God seems absent, the search
> must be for a new authentic meaning which includes
> within itself the new conditions which make that search

necessary. It must be a philosophical and theological search.[15]

Now meaning, unlike truth, is partly made and partly discovered. Further, it is never absent from a human life. Nothing is ever strictly meaningless. When Grant talks about meaning becoming obscure he is expressing dissatisfaction with the trivial and unstable meanings people actually entertain, and with this it is easy to sympathise. It is conceivable that some new, overpowering religion might sweep the world, as Christianity did before it, and install a new moral order in which due and proper limits to man's technological possibility were imposed. Indeed, this is the only thing that would meet Grant's dissatisfaction with the modern world. But it is unlikely, because of the pluralism of modern societies and the end of the conception of the good life. Further, if it were to happen, it would have no necessary implication for philosophy.

There are only two things you can do with philosophy. One is to sweep it aside in the name of practice, as religions have often done, by claiming a revelation from a source far higher than man's unaided reason. This works for a bit, but some species of philosophy usually comes sneaking back after a few centuries, offering itself as a kind of cognitive Jeeves willing to clean up the mess into which the theological Woosters have got themselves. Once readmitted, philosophy has a nasty habit of taking over the whole show, which is what happened during the Middle Ages.

The other thing you can do with philosophy is refute it. But the task of rolling back four centuries of rationalist and empiricist errors is a big one, and Grant, wisely, does not attempt it. He merely restates his Platonism. He points to what are, arguably, the bad social and political consequences of taking certain steps in philosophy, such as setting up the subject-object dichotomy, analysing the meaning of good independently of any metaphysic of final causes, distinguishing facts from values, and so on. But he does not attempt to destroy these philosophical moves, nor indeed to analyse the problem situations within which they arose. This is his weakness as a philosopher, but it may be his strength as a prophet. And it certainly leaves plenty of work for philosophical Grantians to do.

NOTES

1   George Grant, "Thinking about Technology," *Technology and Justice.* (Toronto: House of Anansi Press Limited, 1986), p.19.

2   Ibid., p. 21.

3   Ibid., p. 23.

4   Compare, again, this sentence from "Ideology in Modern Empires": "As discussion of the goodness of ends... has no place in political science, there is no reason within the science why its discoveries about the objective behaviour of human beings should not be at the disposal of wicked men." *Perspectives of Empire: Essays presented to Gerald S. Graham,* edited by John E. Flint and Glyndwr Williams (London: Longman, 1973), p. 194. Since political science must be, like the computer, an inseparable part of our technological question, what is left of this as a criticism of those who have developed empirical political science?

5   Grant, *Philosophy in the Mass Age.* (Toronto: Copp Clark Publishing, 1959), pp. 7-8.

6   Grant, "Thinking about Technology," *Technology and Justice,* pp. 32, 28.

7   Grant, "Faith and the Multiversity," op. cit. *supra,* p. 39.

8   Ibid., p. 51.

9   Michael Oakeshott, *Rationalism in Politics.* (London: Oxford, 1964), pp. 207-208.

10   John Keats, in Oakeshott, op. cit. *supra,* p. 207-8.

11   Grant, *Philosophy in the Mass Age,* p. 26.

12   Grant, "Nietzsche and the Ancients," *Technology and Justice,* p. 94.

13   Grant, "Abortion and Rights," *Technology and Justice,* p. 119.

14   Grant, *Philosophy in the Mass Age,* p. 43.

15   Ibid., p. 7.

TECHNOLOGY AND JUSTICE:
A ROUND TABLE DISCUSSION

Ed Andrew and Zdravko Planinc

Edward Andrew found Kenneth Minogue's scattered attack on George
Grant for the most part misconceived. Minogue's misconstruction is
most evident in his portrait of Grant as a non-philosophic Jeremiah
who rails at technological modernity from some Archimedean point
outside modern history, or from what Minogue conceived as the
standpoint of an Anglican Platonist.[1] This imputed ahistorical and
judgemental standpoint overlooks Grant's openness to concrete experiences of contemporary life. Grant's thought is immersed in the
tasks and benefits of an advanced industrial society. The immersion is
a partial one only because of Grant's accompanying experiences of
deprival, of unsatisfied need, of longing for community or for a
common good to provide order and meaning to our lives. In Andrew's
view, Dennis Lee's position·is truer than the antithetical position of
Minogue. Whereas Minogue presented technological processes as
occurring independently, but before the eyes, of Grant the spectator-
judge, Lee presented Grant as someone who underwent the experience
of living within a technological environment and who reflected on our
experience with categories of thought given us as a legacy of the
technological project of controlling nature and human nature. What
Lee called Grant's impasse is an experience that occurs because technique has dissolved the pre-modern ground of natural law and has left
us groundless, with no firm stance from which to reach forth to what
is good. Lee correctly pointed out that Grant asserted "we are technique,"
and thus we are nothing — nothing other than the techniques of
thinking, loving, and doing that have been given to us.

Minogue rejects what he takes to be Grant's wholesale condemnation of technique. Although unrestrained technology might create
ecological disasters, Minogue thinks that with sufficient political will,

175

such as that of the present British government, humans can use technology rather than be used by it. Thus, the real opposition between Grant and Minogue, Andrew felt, pertains to the question of whether human beings have identifiable purposes independent of modern technological destiny. Grant says "we are technique" and Minogue says "we have technique." To be sure, when one says to another "he has technique," one could imply that the other is nothing but the techniques he employs in his lovemaking, his paper-writing, or whatever. However, Minogue clearly implies that our identities or selves are not constituted by a totality of techniques. The crucial point separating Grant and Minogue pertains to the question of whether our identities are constituted independently of, or by participation in, the world of technology.

Since Minogue rejects the standpoint of an eternal soul uncontaminated by the course of historical events, we may assume that he thinks our selves are constituted by the choices we make amongst the historically bestowed modes of comportment to the modern world. While the quantitative-calculative mode of experience is not insignificant, it is not exhaustive of our world of experience. We do not necessarily experience nature as a resource for consumption; we may instead view nature with pagan delight, or with the reverence of the poet. Thus Minogue implies that we are more than technique, that our identity is instead historically conditioned: but not all the historical conditions limiting our choices are technological in character. Minogue is less concerned than Grant that our practical judgement, our sense of history and of poetry, our loves and our loyalties are swept up in technological imperatives. He is also less concerned that our language — of subjects and objects, values and facts, culture and world views, human and natural resources, freedom of choice and convenience, viable options and impossibility, the necessary and the good — is decisively informed by the technological antithesis of human beings and natural beings and the technological project of humans mastering nature.

Andrew thought that if Minogue had not merely criticized Grant's Platonism but had also provided a positive alternative to Grant's conservatism, he might have made more use of his mentor, Michael Oakeshott. Oakeshott, like Grant, manages to combine both conservatism and thought. However, Oakeshott's conservatism derives more from the tradition of Hume and Burke, whereas Grant's derives from a Platonic rationalism. What Minogue calls Grant's demonology with respect to Descartes and Bacon's aim of the conquest of nature is manifest in Oakeshott's *Rationalism in Politics*. Indeed, Andrew could think of nothing in Grant that was comparable to Oakeshott's ahistorical judgement: *"Je ne puis pardonner à Descartes."* Nevertheless, Andrew thought, Oakeshott is concerned with the way technique dissolves tradition, how the "one best way" of technique tends to undermine the plurality of customary ways of doing things, or how the rationalist problem-solving mentality can sap the nourishment from an historical ethos or life-giving tradition. Grant's thought, unlike Oakeshott's, does not differentiate between technology's assault on an historical ethos and its threatened conquest of nature and human nature. Like Jacques Ellul, Grant thought custom or tradition necessary to human life. Grant and Ellul held that technique, as an enemy of historical continuity or the conservatism of folkways, might thus undercut the possibility of human life, and perhaps even of biological life. In short, Andrew thought that Grant does not differentiate sufficiently between the historical and the ontological aspects of our technological predicament, that is, between technology as a threat to an historical ethos and as an enemy of nature and human nature. The conflation of the historical and the natural is, in Andrew's view, the substance behind Minogue's deprecation of Grant as an Anglican Platonist. Grant's failure to differentiate between the historical and the natural, between the man-made and changeable and the God-made and unchangeable, leaves his readers in the impasse described by Lee, without directions for thought and practice. Perhaps Grant would think the demand for directions is a practical demand that leads us from the one thing needful — contemplation of our present state of being.

Andrew thought that a positive alternative to Grant's conservatism might indicate those elements within our historical ethos that resist the technological pollution of our experience. Perhaps an Oakeshottian (to the extent that he resists monetarist rationalism) would say that the healthy elements of a tradition, or the customs and forms of experience that stand up to, and do not kneel before, global technology and consumerist culture, vary from country to country. Perhaps, Andrew concluded, neither a Platonic nor a Humean conservatism, neither Grant nor Minogue, can relieve us of the necessity of thought. If one thinks that one's traditions can resist the homogenization of cultures by capitalist technology and are able to direct technology towards non-technological objectives, then one's conservatism might be strengthened by Oakeshott's writings. If one finds one's own traditions inadequate to the task of preserving the earth and sky, if traditionalism is unequal to the magnitude of the task of our times, then Grant's rationalism would better nourish our resolve than an ungrounded traditionalism.

Zdravko Planinc agreed with Andrew's assessment of Minogue's paper. He began his remarks by considering one of the fundamental questions raised by Minogue: does Grant give an adequate philosophical account of technology? In contrast to Minogue, Planinc posed the question from the standpoint of Grant's own understanding of philosophy. For Grant, philosophy is an erotic activity directed by the love of God and not by a love of ideas or abstractions. Philosophy is thus closer to prophecy in the Israelite sense than it is to metaphysics, and it has no similarity to ideology. Planinc's answer to the question, posed in Grant's own terms, was no. The best evidence of this was the impasse in Grant's thought described by Lee. Nevertheless, said Planinc, Grant's work is significant because of the way it illuminates the origins of this impasse and the difficulty of overcoming it.

Grant's impasse may result from his attempt to "think what technology *is*." By thinking in this way, Grant tries to determine the ontological status of technology, or the being of technology and its place in the order of being. This cannot be done, Planinc claimed, because technology has no ontological status. Only things that have existence in the order of being can be "thought" philosophically, just as only such things can be loved. But Grant's thinking about technology is not simply based on an error. It is also an attempt to understand the spiritual condition that allows for the existence of technological society or modernity. Technology claims ontological status for itself — or rather, some people make this claim on its behalf. When Grant "thinks what technology *is*," therefore, he is actively participating in the spiritual condition that defines modernity. This activity is not fruitless since spiritual conditions do have ontological status and can be assessed comparatively. However, it leads Grant to an impasse because it compels him to accept as true the modern opinion that technology is all-encompassing and definitive of human existence. Planinc said that, although existence in technological society constitutes the predominant part of our lived experience today, the claim that it is the totality of human experience is simply false. Grant understood that technology is not exhaustive of our experience, but he often had difficulty putting his understanding into words.

Planinc then discussed the nature of Grant's impasse in different terms. He based his remarks on a passage from Friedrich Nietzsche's *Will to Power* (749), in which the voice of the nihilist says:

> The charm that works for us, the Venus eye that fascinates even our foes and blinds them, is the magic of the extreme, the seductive force that radiates from all that is utmost.[2]

When Grant attempts to think what technology is, he allows himself to be seduced by the magical extreme of modernity, the extreme capable of blinding foes as formidable as Grant. It is necessary to allow oneself to be so seduced, Planinc claimed, if one is to cultivate a truly philosophic *eros* in the modern world. However, this magical seduction is blinding because it undermines the common sense on which philosophy is founded. Planinc defined common sense as the type of rationality and spirituality that is relatively unreflective and yet aware of all the basic features of human existence within the order of being. The best historical example of the social predominance of common sense, he said, is the British Christian commonwealth of which Grant is such a profound representative. On its own, common sense can be mulish, but it can also be developed into philosophy and theology informed by the love of God. The first difficulty Grant encounters in his attempt to cultivate this type of *eros* is the erosion of common sense by the social predominance of the spiritual condition typical of modernity. Grant finds it necessary to allow himself to be seduced by modernity's magical extreme for two reasons: to preserve common sense itself; and to live through the experience in order to become a philosopher. The seduction itself, therefore, produces only an apparent impasse. Grant's true impasse originates in his gnosticism. Planinc said Grant's reason for turning to *gnosis* is understandable. The empty metaphysical speculation that comprises the greatest part of modern philosophy and theology has little to do with the *eros* evident in the Platonic dialogues and the synoptic Gospels. The intellectual and spiritual *gnosis* Grant found in the works of Leo Strauss and Simone Weil provided him with an alternative to unerotic modern philosophy and theology. However, the alternative they provided was different from the one he was seeking. Even though they seem similar, *gnosis* and the highly erotic mystical experiences Grant sought are essentially different in character. The difference between them is evident in their respective abilities to resist and even overcome the seductive power of modernity. Planinc said that Grant understood the most important characteristic of modernity or technological society to be the activist gnosticism that lies at its heart. Grant attempted to cultivate the highest forms of *eros* in order to resist the seductive power of such magical extremism. However, the intellectual and spiritual gnosticism to which Grant was drawn was unable to resist it. Contemplative gnosticism provides no effective alternative to activist gnosticism. Instead, they confirm one another, and this impasse, Planinc concluded, is the most serious barrier in Grant's thinking about technology.

Peter Self compared Grant and Minogue by means of Isaiah Berlin's *The Hedgehog and the Fox*. Berlin's fox who knows a great many little things is Ken Minogue, while Berlin's hedgehog who knows only one big thing is George Grant. Self considered himself foxy in temperament like Minogue and questioned whether Grant knew what the big thing was anyway. He shared Minogue's belief that in the contemporary world one cannot ground concepts of justice in revealed religion or classical political thought. He found the moral intuitionism of G. E. Moore an adequate grounding for thoughts about justice. Although Minogue demurred, Self maintained that goodness is like the colour green: you may be unable to define it precisely, but you know it when you see it. He said he would leave the grounds of justice to moral philosophers, as he was confident that he knew what was just and unjust in specific public policy initiatives he had studied in recent years.

Observing that the concept of technological society was extremely complex, Self wished that Grant, Minogue, Andrew or Planinc had clarified it to his satisfaction, or at least attempted to unpack the hold-all concept of technology. Whether or not Grant assumed that science and technology were inextricably intertwined, science, Self asserted, is still concerned with the age-old quest for truth, while technology is concerned with controlling or manipulating the environment. Grant was wrong to think that pursuing the Platonic trinity of truth, goodness and beauty is difficult in a technological society. Truth is a matter of attitude, a willingness to know the truth however uncomfortable it may be. Self took the side of Darwin who, despite his religious convictions, overturned a cosy cosmology in the search for truth. The pursuit of truth is not implicated in, but rather is stimulated by, technological development.

Self recounted his educational experiences at English public schools and at Oxford to indicate that, since technology is not uniformly spread through society, the idea of a technological society is an oversimplification. Educational establishments were generally located far from industry, lacked the most elementary technological amenities, and emphasized a classical education, not technical training. He cited the great Balliol classicist, Benjamin Jowett, as saying, "What do the undergraduates want baths for? They're only up here for eight weeks."

Self indicated the dominance of Kantian philosophy while he and Grant were at Oxford: A. D. Lindsay, E. Cassirer, A. H. Smith, M. Kemp Smith and A. Paton were all lecturing on Kant. Grant was strongly influenced by Kant, and remained so even after he accepted Nietzsche's dictum that Kant, was "the great delayer" of secular modernity. Self acknowledged that, for Kant, the good is constituted by the creative moral will, whereas for Grant, the good is discovered by the intelligence. Yet Grant shared Kant and Self's notion of human equality, in the sense of an equal entitlement to care, compassion and concern, and in the sense of equal provision of public services and opportunities. Another Kantian conception that informed Grant's thought was the sense of awe; the unknowable awesomeness of the world prevents hubris, or supports the notion of the moral equality of human beings. Balancing this literal element was Grant's conservative respect for established expectations and traditions, for the stability they bring, and for the ordinary man's view that one should not disrupt these expectations too lightly.

Self indicated that he is a "green" and shares Grant's concern about the unlimited exploitation of nature for the sake of human comfort. He thought the hubris of unlimited manipulation of the

181

environment and the belief in a technical solution to all problems is most prevalent in North America. The fantastic dreams of "Star Wars" and the claims of psychiatrists to be able to treat evil by means of psychological massage provide some warrant for Grant's concern. Self pointed out that one of Grant's favourite phrases is "the Marxism of the U.S.A.," connoting the sin of hubris. Indeed, he said, Rainer Knopff is correct in maintaining that Grant disliked liberal capitalism even more than Marxism. Self explained that liberal capitalism is destructive of the values of stability and parochialism in which Grant believed. Its dominant ethos is the expectation that everything changes with technological progress and moves with capital investments; the values of family, locality, and stability of expectation are dissolved by the flow of capital. On this point, Self emphatically sided with Grant. He cited empirical studies to show that, at least in the developed world, the happiest people are found in the least economically developed areas; among the British, the happiest are found in the north of England and Scotland, while in Canada, the Newfoundlanders are happiest. It is evident that the underdeveloped world hates being poor, but development is less of a boon once basic subsistence is provided.

Self believed that the fundamental failing of most political philosophers, including Grant and all the commentators at the conference, was the failure to take public choice theory seriously. Public choice theory, which Self has criticized in two books, is an American "free enterprise philosophy" that is corrupting civil servants around the globe. If political philosophers would descend from their ethereal heights, he said, they might have something to contribute to the formation of social and political policy. In the absence of any such descent to the mundane, public choice theorists such as James Buchanan will have a free field in which to propound their market model of the common good as an aggregate of individual desires. This model implicitly assumes that the common good is nothing other than the maximization of marketable and individually consumable goods and services. Those who share Grant's moral concerns, Self concluded, would do well to read public choice theory and then elaborate a philosophic basis, independent of any revealed religion, for a concept of justice that will confront the dominant doctrines shaping social and political policies.

James Wiser prefaced his remarks by indicating that the difference between Minogue's reading of Grant's works and his own is based on their differing understandings of the essential concerns of political philosophy. Wiser shared Grant's view that the question about the nature of the good life is central to political philosophy. Grant's attempt to answer this question is particularly thought-provoking in that it intends to combine two traditions, the classical Greek and the modern.

The classical political philosophers discuss the good life in terms of justice and virtue. The moderns discuss it in terms of interests, desires and needs. Both traditions have their own strengths and weaknesses. In particular, the classical concern for justice and virtue pays insufficient attention to the realm of economic and productive activity. On the other hand, the modern concern for the interests, wants and desires expressed in this realm of activity pays insufficient attention to questions of justice and virtue; indeed, the modern tradition originates in a self-conscious effort to establish a radically new foundation for society requiring no reference to classical concerns. Wiser said that Grant attempts to combine the strengths of both traditions. Grant rethinks the classical Greek concern for justice and virtue while keeping at the center of his thought a deep recognition of the importance of the productive and practical realm.

Wiser then remarked that other contemporary thinkers have made similar attempts to address the question of the good life, often presenting the issue in terms of a debate between ancients and moderns. There is, however, a basic problem with their approach that Grant, for the most part, avoids. They understand the debate between the ancients and moderns as a contest of doctrines or ideas. They assume, therefore, that the problems of modernity can be resolved at the level of doctrine or ideas. For them, it is necessary only to learn to think correctly or to change one's mind. In contrast, Grant understands that the issue must be addressed at a deeper, experiential level.

Wiser said the deeper question to which Grant addresses himself is, how can we once again apprehend and trust our intimations of a promised meaning that necessarily escapes our explicit formulations and logical proofs? This is not a doctrinal matter. It concerns a lack of experience, or rather, a lack of social affirmation and accreditation of certain experiences. Grant states this quite clearly when he writes:

> Nevertheless, it may, perhaps, be said negatively that what has been absent for us is the affirmation of a possible apprehension of the world beyond that as a field of objects considered as pragmata — an apprehension present not only in its heights as 'theory' but as the undergirding of our loves and friendships, of our arts and reverences, and indeed as the setting for our dealing with the objects of the human and non-human world.[3]

The problem is the ability to apprehend, to apperceive, to experience. Grant makes a similar point when, in the context of a larger discussion of faith, love and beauty, he writes:

> The old teaching was that we love otherness, not because it is other, but because it is beautiful. The beauty of others was believed to be an experience open to everyone, though in extraordinarily different forms, and at differing steps towards perfection.... The beauty of otherness is the central assumption in the statement, 'Faith is the experience that the intelligence is enlightened by love.'[4]

Wiser understood this passage to indicate that our statements are founded upon experiences and that we cannot ground our statements unless we somehow affirm the experiences they assume.

Wiser concluded that Grant's analysis of and response to modernity does not concern itself with doctrines. It addresses more fundamental questions. How did we lose our ability to apperceive? More precisely, why are apperceptions of beauty, truth and love — experiences which people do have — no longer socially authoritative? Grant does not assume that the proper response to these questions is a matter of changing one's mind either individually or in common with others. Rather, it is necessary that we develop the ability once again to accredit such experiences in an environment that denies their legitimacy.

In contrast to Minogue's claim that Grant's critique of modernity is expressed from an Archimedean point outside his own society, Tom Darby agreed with Andrew that the distinctive feature of Grant's thought is its rootedness. It is a rootedness related to the philosophic *eros*, but it is nonetheless a rootedness in modern society. This is evident in *Technology and Empire*, where Grant writes:

> To exist as a North American is an amazing and enthralling fate. As in every historical condition, some not only have to live their fate, but also to let it come to be thought. What we have built and become in so short a time calls forth amazement in the face of its novelty, an amazement which leads to that thinking. Yet the very dynamism of the novelty enthralls us to inhibit that thinking.[5]

Grant both lives the fate of his society and lets it come to be thought. Furthermore, Darby said, he invites us, indeed implores us, to think it as well. In particular, he asks us to think our technology and our justice together.

Darby referred to a passage from *English-Speaking Justice* that he considered a good example of Grant's way of thinking these things together:

> Our justice is being played out within a destiny more comprehensive than itself. A quick name for this is 'technology.' I mean by that word the endeavour which summons forth everything (both human and non-human) to give its reasons.... It has been said that communism and contractual capitalism are predicates of the subject technology. They are ways in which our comprehensive destiny is lived out. But clearly that technological destiny has its own dynamic conveniences, which easily sweep away our tradition of justice, if the latter gets in the way.[6]

In reference to Lee's discussion of Grant's impasse, Darby described Grant's thinking in this passage as an Hegelian *Umweg* or detour; detours in thought sometimes result in an impasse. To understand why

Grant takes this detour one must consider what he means by the term "destiny."

For Grant, technology is our destiny. It is that which we do not question; it is the most authoritative thing in modern society. Darby distinguished destiny from providence and fate. While destiny is not blind, as is fate, it also has no *telos*, unlike providence. Destiny, for Grant, is similar to the pre-Socratic understanding of *moira* as that which binds us. In Greek tragedy and in Homer's epics, when mortals trespass to a great degree, no god in the pantheon can save them from their destiny. They are given a destiny at the same time as they live their destiny. Both receiving and living a destiny may be said to occur when mortals trespass the boundary established by justice, the measure of their actions. However, the modern destiny is not bound by justice. Boundless technology has become the measure of our society, the form of our justice and the essence of our destiny.

Darby disagreed with Minogue's assessment of Grant as a philosopher and a prophet. Minogue was correct to describe Grant in this way, but correct for the wrong reasons. As a philosopher, Grant took his measure from the Greeks; in the imagery of Plato's cave allegory, philosophy for Grant was an erotic ascent, not the cool contemplation of the heavens. And yet Grant's thought remains rooted. He does not attempt to leave the cave or the city behind. Instead, he returns to it because it is his home. In more contemporary terms, Grant recognized that the realm of the heavens no longer provide a measure for man, or a boundary he must not trespass. The cosmos is no longer understood as evidence of a natural law. St. Thomas' account of the four types of law, Darby claimed, does not help us understand the nature of Grant's philosophy. What is perhaps most helpful in Thomas' writing is his warning that the rational and erotic parts of our nature must not be divorced. Grant agreed with Thomas that *eros* illuminates *ratio* in our discernment of justice. *Ratio* divorced from *eros* tends to become calculating rationality, as it has done in modernity. *Eros* not only illuminates our pursuit of substantial justice; *eros* also graces formal justice, or provides the mercy that tempers it.

Darby compared Grant to Socrates as a prophet in the philosophic sense. Grant's rootedness in, but criticism of, his own society recalls Socrates' similar relation to his city. At the end of the *Apology*,

Socrates curses his accusers, and yet he asks them to treat his children as he had treated them and their children. As well, Grant's way of thinking, motivated by philosophic *eros*, recalls the description Socrates gives in the *Phaedo* of philosophy as the practice of dying. In addition, Darby concluded, Grant is also a prophet in the biblical sense. In this, he most resembles Jeremiah. Grant is a prophet in that he speaks for, and stands in for, and is one of, a remnant. Grant perhaps speaks for a remnant of humanity. He certainly speaks for a remnant in *Lament for a Nation*. However, the prophetic remarks of his *Lament* are not addressed to Canadians alone. They concern this nation, but they also concern the common things that underlie all nations — nativity and common origins — and how these common things are affected by technology. The prophecy of the *Lament*, therefore, is addressed to those of us who live in Canada, to those of us who live in North America, and to those of us who dwell in terror and in wonder of the twentieth century.

NOTES

1 Minogue did not spell out the incongruity of Plato and contemporary Anglicanism. One may infer that Grant thought Plato could reveal important truths to contemporaries, whether Anglican or not, whereas Minogue is doubtful whether Plato's reflections on his historical experience would have much relevance to contemporaries.

2 Translation by Eric Voegelin in his "Wisdom and the Magic of the Extreme," *Southern Review*, n.s. 17 (1981), p. 243.

3 George Grant, "In Defence of North America," *Technology and Empire — Perspectives on North America*. (Toronto: House of Anansi Press Limited, 1969), p. 35.

4 Grant, "Faith and the Multiversity," *Technology and Justice*. (Toronto: House of Anansi Press Limited, 1986), p. 39.

5 Grant, "In Defence of North America," *Technology and Empire*, p. 15.

6 George Grant, *English-Speaking Justice*. (Sackville: Mount Allison University, 1974), p. 88.

THE MAGIC OF ART

William Christian

> About the magic of the art in which
> the dance of this prodigality
> is achieved — well, it is magic, and I
> cannot speak of it here and perhaps
> not at all.[1]
>
> George Grant

When I first discovered that I was to appear on the same programme as two such distinguished artists as Dennis Lee and Alex Colville, I was delighted. But as I reflected on the matter, I became more perplexed. I knew what I was doing here, but why were they here too? I represented philosophy, the greatest and most comprehensive gift of the Muses, whereas they stood merely for poetry and painting. Not only had these activities been banished from the ideal life described in the *Republic*, but in the *Phaedrus* the poet and the other artists who imitated the world of the senses were assigned only the sixth most attractive life, after the businessman, the athlete and the prophet, and just ahead of the artisan and farmer.[2]

As tempting as it was to view the programme merely as an example of Peter Emberley's catholic tastes and culture, I was nagged by the recollection that Grant had dedicated *English-Speaking Justice*, the work which I consider his most sustained piece of philosophic thinking, to Alex Colville and Dennis Lee — "two artists who have taught me about justice." This seemed a strangely un-Platonic way to begin.

The more I thought about it, the more enigmatic this dedication became. How had these two men taught Grant about justice? He once told me that he had learned much about justice from Arthur, his dog. This I understood, thanks to Plato, who reminded us that one aspect of justice was helping our friends and harming our enemies; and loyalty

189

is surely characteristic of our canine companions. Perhaps it was in an analogous way that Lee and Colville had taught him. For instance, he was always grateful to Dennis Lee for the reception he got for his collection of essays *Technology and Empire*, after the difficulties he had had finding a publisher for *Lament for a Nation*. Was this perhaps the kind of thing he had learned from them — the low but sustaining kind of justice as fair-dealing that one encounters from time to time in business arrangements of various sorts ?

Grant had dedicated others of his books to friends or relations: "To Derek Bedson and Judith Robinson, Two Lovers of Their Country, One Living and One Dead"; to "William, who taught me about Nietzsche." Perhaps it was in this vein that he was considering Colville and Lee, since they were both men about whom he cared and whose friendship had enriched his life. Plato explores this question in the *Lysis*, where he points out to two young men that they can only truly be friends in the communion of some shared good. That thought seemed promising but not persuasive. Derek Bedson and Judith Robinson, a public servant and a journalist, were friends too, but they merited their dedication by dint of their patriotism. William is his son, but the dedication was apt because William when young had encountered the writings of Nietzsche in a profound and powerful way that awakened Grant to the fact that Nietzsche enucleated the core of modernity. It could not, then, be just as friends that these two had taught Grant about justice; it was their capacity as artists that he learned from them. Must the contemporary philosopher sit at the feet of the poets and the painters? This became the pressing question.

Grant had been concerned from his earliest important work, *Philosophy in the Mass Age*, with the possibility that through art man could escape from the more serious problems in which modernity had entangled him.[3] Under the influence of Hegel, Grant accepted the view that art shared with philosophy and religion the potential to comprehend and articulate the coherence of the whole. In the great writers of the past, art was revealed as "the instrument of a truth beyond us,"[4] and at the highest level of sophistication, that of the great Greek plays, art achieved a "mythic consciousness."[5] Nonetheless, the artist's achievements and the philosopher's were inherently different, though they complemented one another. "Only a great artist could state this affirmation in the concrete; only a great philosopher could show it can withstand any argument brought against it."[6]

In contrast to the rich mythical textures of antiquity the modern world is a hollow and sterile thing in which entertainment "is used to keep people happy by identifying life as it is with life as it ought to be. Art is used to enfold us in the acceptance of what we are."[7] For this state of affairs modern philosophy is primarily responsible,[8] because it has cut man off from the past and isolated him entirely within the historicist assumptions of his own age. To escape from this sterile enfolding requires an exercise of the historical imagination so as to work through to a sympathetic understanding of ages in which moral presuppositions differed fundamentally from those which encircle us today. This imaginative effort is necessary even to attain the first step in the process, which is the mere awareness that we are constricted by the horizons of modernity.[9]

The liberating power of art could be seen, Grant thought, in the decision of the Chinese and Russian regimes to condemn rock-and-roll as decadent, because even this form of musical expression revealed "an attempt of the young to express themselves on a level beyond the practical."[10] This was, of course, merely a flicker compared to the power of great art to enlighten the whole. "Insofar as artists come to take their art seriously and try to think and practise it within a fuller perspective," Grant thought at this point, "...the contradictions of our present practice may yet be overcome."[11] However, in order to play this role the artist must use his leisure for activities "which have as their ends joy rather than power, adoration rather than control."[12] This is the character of true art, and it is this element which places it beyond the obsessive concern with material production and domination. Consequently, Grant argues that the Hegelian triad of artist, philosopher, and mystic "have been outsiders in our Protestant civilization."[13]

Coincidentally, *Outsiders* was the title of a book by Hans Meyer which Grant reviewed in 1982, a work which, because of its historicist assumptions, it was appropriate to describe as "out of date." Such could never be an appropriate description for the older traditional understanding of art. "It is, of course, foolish to use the phrase 'out of date' about writers such as Plato or Tolstoy, who are telling us what is true of all times and places."[14]

Between the first appearance of *Philosophy in the Mass Age* and the publication of this review, Grant had changed his mind on several important philosophical questions. What had happened in between was decisive for his thought. As he wrote in his introduction to the 1966 edition of *Philosophy in the Mass Age*:

> ... I came to the conclusion that Hegel was not correct in his claim to have taken the truth of antique thought and synthesized it with the modern to produce a higher (and perhaps highest) truth; that on many of the most important political matters Plato's teaching is truer than Hegel's. Particularly, I have come to the conclusion that Plato's account of what constitutes human excellence and the possibility of its realization in the world is more valid than that of Hegel.[15]

Now, one might expect that this conversion to Platonism, influenced in part by the writings of Simone Weil, would dramatically alter Grant's view of the role of the artist. But I shall argue here that this was not the case. Grant retained throughout the Hegelian notion that the artistic vision was a comprehensive insight into the whole, complementary to the philosopher's vision.

To make this point it is necessary first to look at Plato's understanding of the role of the artist. Although there are ambiguities in Plato's account, it is generally taken as true that he held artists in low esteem for two main reasons. The first is that the epiphanies which illuminate the artist often come from a contemplation of the transitory things of this world. The paintings of Van Gogh, for example, can illuminate the objects of ordinary domestic life such as those in his room in Arles, but this sort of imitative art is a totally unsatisfactory medium for conveying the truth about the unchanging realities which are visible only through the eye of the soul.

The second inadequacy of artists is that they are often unable to defend their creations from criticism. When Socrates approached the poets in the *agora*, he found that they were incapable of elucidating their own creations. The words might speak for themselves, but their authors were incapable of subjecting them to rigorous and sustained criticism or of explicating them satisfactorily when others did so. Like Ion in Plato's early dialogue, they were usually reduced to reiteration.

Consequently it was characteristic of artists that those who were truly inspired by the gods could not be distinguished from those who merely practised a craft without divine inspiration. Even worse, it was sometimes hard to separate those whose madness was divine from those who suffered from a more mundane, demotic craziness.

For Plato, then, it was only the philosopher who could adequately judge the creations of the artists, since he alone was in a position to assess the adequacy of their representations of the changeless world of the ideal. Moreoover, only he could clarify their meaning through dialectic, sorting out inadequate from more comprehensive understandings.

It is therefore somewhat surprising to find Grant continuing to emphasize the role of the artist in his essays after he had come to the conclusion that the writings of Plato were the philosophical works most in accord with the vision of existence which had been vouchsafed to him by the faith he acquired in his conversion to a transcendental understanding of Christianity. However, in the face of a science which concluded that "we are accidental inhabitants of a negligible planet in the endless spaces," he continued to claim for art a redemptive power, because:

> ...men are forced to seek meaning in other ways than through the intellect. If truth leads to meaninglessness, then men in their thirst for meaning turn to art. To hope to find in the products of the imagination that meaning which has been cast out of the intellect may, in the light of Socrates, be known to be a fruitless quest. Nevertheless, it is a thirst which is the enemy of tyranny.[16]

The position that Grant adopts here is that the fragmentation of the modern consciousness has made it difficult, even impossible, for the philosopher to play his proper role — that of explaining the wholeness of the good and the goodness of the whole.[17] As Grant said in his 1974 Wood lectures, subsequently published as *English-Speaking Justice*: "This lack of a tradition of thought is one reason why it is improbable that the transcendence of justice over technology will be lived among the English-speaking people."[18] Yet in spite of these reservations, it must be remembered that Grant spoke merely of the improbability, not the impossibility of living the transcendence of justice in the modern world. This position is fully consistent with that enunciated in 1969 in "A Platitude," the concluding essay in *Technology and Empire*. There Grant writes that

> it would be immoderate and uncourageous and perhaps unwise to live in the midst of our present drive, merely working in it and celebrating it, and not also listening or watching or simply waiting for intimations of deprival which might lead us to see the beautiful as the image, in the world, of the good.[19]

Or, as he had put it in his article on the university curriculum:

> Although that sustainment cannot be adequately thought by us because of the fragmentation and complexity of our historical inheritance, this is still no reason not to open ourselves to all those occasions in which the reality of that sustaining makes itself present to us.[20]

Here Grant can be seen adopting the Platonic position most beautifully expressed in *Phaedrus*, that we are drawn to the good through our perception of and love for the beauty that we find in the world and perceive through our senses, particularly sight. In order to be aware of this beauty, we have to hold in abeyance the forces of modern rationalism which issue forth in technology. Should we manage to do so, we might be able to gain an insight into the transcendent world by a means other than faith. We might be able to achieve a poetic insight into the nature of transcendence. Grant was later to offer Mozart as the most perfect example of this phenomenon, the beloved of God who "says that after composing a piece of music he sees it 'all in one look' and when he says he understands it all at one moment, he is surely describing an act which can properly be named 'intellectual intuition'."[21]

To clarify this notion of "intellectual intuition," Grant drew on the Platonic theory of knowledge as recollection. In his mythical presentation of this theory, Plato suggests that all souls, before they were embodied, had knowledge of the eternal and transcendent reality, but just prior to embodiment they were washed in the river Lethe, or Forgetfulness. The knowledge which they enjoy in this world, then, is the consequence of recollecting what has once been known and then subsequently forgotten. It is some such position, I think, which lies beneath Grant's comments about the Countess' air *Dove sono*: "In Mozart's great threnody, the Countess sings of *la memoria di quel bene*. One cannot argue the meaninglessness of the world from the facts of evil, because what could evil deprive us of, if we had not some prior knowledge of good?"[22]

After the publication of *Lament*, Grant was often described as a pessimist, a term with which he was uncomfortable not least for etymological reasons. However, following the Roe v. Wade decision of the American Supreme Court he began genuinely to despair about the future of his civilization. "The darkness is fearful, because what is at stake is whether anything is good."[23] He found himself to be a little like Kurt Vonnegut's hero in *Sirens of Titan* (1959): his space ship had broken down billions of miles from earth, and help was not on the way. Little succour, he thought, could be expected from the universities or from other contemporary thinkers because the modern project had gone inherently awry.

> Analytic logistics plus historicist scholarship plus even rigorous science do not when added up equal philosophy. When added together they are not capable of producing that thought which is required if justice is to be taken out of the darkness which surrounds it in the technological era.[24]

The student revolt of the 1960s and the opposition to the Vietnam war had given Grant a glimmer of encouragement. He saw in the young what he described as "a hunger and thirst for ecstatic relations which transcend the contractual."[25] However, these intimations had two severe limitations. First, they tended to the private sphere rather than the public and were manifested most enthusiastically in sexual relations. Second, the young showed a dangerous fascination for Eastern religions, especially in a vulgarized form which brought them close to nihilism. These flights from the aridity of contractual liberalism simply did not have the sustaining power to reverse the drive of technological dynamism. *Lament for a Nation* had further argued that the distinctive society which had been formed in

British North America no longer enjoyed the autonomy to pursue a rival vision of the good. Whence was redemption to come?

As Grant wrote in a book review, since "the decay of philosophy and theology, literature has become the means whereby the educated masses are being introduced to many forms of knowledge which may not be given through the study of modern sciences."[26] This view of the significance of literature as a possible source of salvation from the crisis of modernity led him to Celine, the twentieth-century French novelist whose significance for our century is comparable to Shakespeare's for the sixteenth. Celine was an odd and controversial choice. Both inside and outside France he was virtually ignored because he had written anti-semitic pamphlets during the 1930s, and was widely thought to have collaborated with the Nazis during the occupation, even though he had been formally cleared of charges of collaboration. As the War reached its end. he fled France in the company of his wife, a French film star, Le Vig, and one of the most memorable animals in the history of literature — Celine's cat Bebert. This odyssey ended with Celine in solitary confinement in Denmark before he was returned to face his now- victorious enemies from the French Resistance.

The last novel of his great trilogy (*Castle to Castle, North* and *Rigadoon*) was finished in 1961, the year of Celine's death. According to Grant:

> [by]the time Celine is writing this trilogy in the 1950s he is all political passion spent. His hopes have been burnt out of him by prison and persecution, by poverty and by age. The splendor of his art lays before us Europe's collapse. Indeed, the very high splendor of his art is somehow related to the fact that his hopes have been burnt out...[27]

As for Celine's disreputable politics, Grant asks for sympathetic understanding on the grounds that "western thought and traditions lie in ruins," and that artists who are "subject to the confusions of the age" should "be more than usually excused."[28] This, however, is a curious defence. Either Celine knows what he is talking about and his vision is clear, or he is merely another scribbler, and certainly not of the first rank to be compared with Shakespeare or Tolstoy.

However, there was another aspect of art which was important for Grant. He had faulted the literary critic Said because he had not explained the magic of Celine's prose. "This takes me back to enrapturing. What I want to know from professors of literature is why Celine is enrapturing."[29]

This is, I think, exactly the point that Grant made all through his writings on the subject of art. Great art has, in his view, a mystical quality which lifts us out of the morass of historicism and positivism. Those who "devote themselves to practice" have to get on with the job and this means that they cannot ever see life whole. "This is why poets and philosophers know they are always in conflict with the workings of society, however much they must try to hide this fact. They must try to see life whole, but parts of that whole can hardly leave them steady."[30] But does this argument not bring us back to the Platonic criticism? How can we distinguish between mere craziness and divine madness if we ourselves are not philosophers?

Grant returned to this question in "Faith and the Multiversity,"[31] the essay which he considered his strongest positive statement. There he addresses the problem directly: "...are there some works that are more worth paying attention to than others? What is given in those that are most worthy of attention?"[32] And he defines enrapturement by asking: "Can we describe that enrapturing as the immediate engrossment in the beauty of the work, which points to good which is quite unrepresentable?"[33]

Why does this not take us back to the core of the Platonic position? How do we know which works of art point us to the ineffable good and which do not? Unless we have philosophy, it seems, we are completely at a loss. What is called modern philosophy has been so fragmented and so misdirected that it is not even heading in the appropriate direction. And if the significance of art lies merely in the experience of rapture, what do we say about those misguided Frenchmen of the 1930s who might be presumed to have been enchanted and even enraptured by Celine's anti-semitic ravings?

There is a further problem with the theory which Grant advanced, but in this case it is one of which Grant was clearly aware. This came from the "modern disjunction between the true and the beautiful."[34] Here, one might say, Grant clearly means that what is experienced as beautiful in the modern world by sensitive souls is not what is thought true by the most respected scientists and philosophers. Is beauty true because it is beautiful, or are there two separate forms, the beautiful and the true? Are all beautiful things true, and are there some truths that lack beauty? The unicorn in the Cluny tapestries is unquestionably beautiful, but what does this say of its ontological status?

Grant was troubled by the difficulties he found in explaining the relation of art to philosophy. As he said to me in our last formal conversation:

> I think [Leo] Strauss is right in saying that the highest argument in Plato is the argument between the poets and the philosophers. In some sense Christianity has exalted the poets as against the philosophers. Of course in the modern world it's gone crazy with Heidegger and Nietzsche. You see it in the whole democratic world. Art and entertainment is everything. There is nothing beyond it. That is a very extraordinary position; that's taking the modern position to its extremity. I think one of the central [ideas is] that art is for Plato *mimesis*, imitation; in the modern world they talk about it as creation. The more atheist they get, the more they take the language of creation. I would love to work this out. It seems to me that something has gone wrong when you say art is creation, as against imitation. I just haven't got round to it. I'm just coming to these things.[35]

I think that Grant was aware of the anomalies of his position and was just coming to think them through. He has, for almost thirty years, held onto the Hegelian image of the dialectical co-operation of the artist and the philosopher in enunciating the wholeness of existence. He continued to believe that truly great artists such as Mozart were capable, through a process described as intellectual intuition, of grasping the healing and true thought that there is a whole, and that this whole is good. How to hold the fact of Mozart together with the arguments of Plato and with the truth about Being which had come to him through faith — this would have been the next great subject of his meditations had his fragile humanity not put an end to his quest.[36]

To Alex Colville, the author of *Lament for a Nation* seemed like a wolf howling in the wilderness. Dennis Lee saw a big, rumpled, sensitive man whose soul suffered from his acute awareness of the impasse our civilization had reached. Barry Cooper found it difficult to know just what sort of creature George Grant was — a scholar, a philosophical labourer, a contemplative, a climber of high and dangerous mountains. In Ken Minogue's view, Grant combines the characteristics of a philosopher with those of a prophet, and his message is that of the strangest of hybrids, the Anglican Platonist. For Joan O'Donovan, Grant was a Christian advocate; he had, in a strange way, returned to his original vocation as a lawyer, but this time his brief was an indictment of the modern world on the charge that it had, like Satan's angels, rebelled against its Creator's law.

I would like to suggest another description which, for me at least, is more compelling than any of the others. I think of Grant as a singer of enchanted songs, of the sort that scare away the *mormolukeia*, the frightful apparitions that flit about in the darkness, particularly that night which envelops our civilization. In the sixties we were soothed by *Lament for a Nation* because it hinted that we could, personally if not collectively, ward off the technologizing liberalism of the American dynamo. In the seventies he reassured us that we could still contemplate technological civilization "in relation to the eternal fire which flames forth in the Gospels and blazes even in the presence of that determining power."[37] And in the 1980s he continued to sing his love songs: "Fire has always been the word to describe love, and it has been written that flame touches flame. The making of a beautiful piece is an act of love, a love which illuminates the lucidity in his making of it."[38]

So we end up in the same position as the friends who surrounded Socrates as he awaited the jailer whose drug would put an end to the enchanted singer's life. They were frightened and sought his reassurance:

CEBES: Where, Socrates, shall we find a good singer of such charms since you are forsaking us?

SOCRATES: Great is Hellas, Cebes, and there are, I suppose, many good men in it; many also are the foreign peoples. You must search through all of these,

199

seeking such a singer of charms. Do not use your
money or your efforts sparingly, for there is nothing of
which you have a greater need on which to spend your
resources. It is also necessary to seek among each other,
for you would probably not easily find anyone better
able to do these things than yourselves.[39]

NOTES

1   From "Celine: Art and Politics," *Queen's Quarterly*, 90/3 (Autumn 1983),
     p. 804.

2   Plato, *Phaedrus*, 248de.

3   Joan O'Donovan in her study, *George Grant and the Twilight of Justice*,
     (Toronto: University of Toronto Press, 1984), does not discuss the
     relationship of art to philosophy at all.

4   George Grant, *Philosophy in the Mass Age*. (Toronto: Copp Clark
     Publicshing, 1959), p. 8.

5   Ibid., p. 19.

6   Ibid., p. 101. In his contribution to the Massey *Commission*, Grant had
     written: "The contemplative life, whether mystical, artistic or philo-
     sophic, has therefore been encouraged by societies not only for the good
     of the contemplative himself but because his influence upon more active
     members was considered of value. Philosophy was therefore encouraged
     as the rational form of such contemplation." George Grant, "Philosophy,"
     Royal Commission on National Development in the Arts, Letters and Sciences.
     (Ottawa: King's Printer, 1951), p. 119.

7   Grant, *Philosophy in the Mass Age*, p. 8.

8   Ibid., p. viii.

9   Ibid., p. 26.

10   Ibid., p. 75.

11   Ibid., p. 111.

12   Ibid., p. 87.

13   Ibid.

14   *Globe and Mail*, October 16, 1982, p. 16.

15   Grant, *Philosophy in the Mass Age*, p. viii.

16   George Grant, *Technology and Empire — Perspectives on North America*. (Toronto: House of Anansi Press Limited, 1969), p. 127.

17   "And God saw everything He had made, and, behold, it *was* very good." (Genesis 1:31.)

18   George Grant, *English-Speaking Justice*. (Sackville, NB: Mount Allison University, 1974), p. 96. The Wood lectures were delivered by Grant but revised for publication, and the work first appeared in 1977, although it is dated 1974.

19   George Grant, "A Platitude," in *Technology and Empire*, p. 143.

20   Grant, "The University Curriculum," op.cit. *supra*, p. 133.

21   George Grant, "Faith and the Multiversity," *Technology and Justice*, (Toronto: House of Anansi Press Limited, 1986), p. 49.

22   George Grant, *Lament for A Nation — The Defeat of Canadian Nationalism*. (Toronto: McClelland & Stewart, 1965), p. 3.

23   Grant, *English-Speaking Justice*, p. 93.

24   Ibid., pp. 95-96.

25   Ibid., p. 12.

26   George Grant, "Review of Edward W. Said, *The World, the Text and the Critic*," *Globe and Mail*, (1983).

27   Grant, "Celine: Art and Politics," p. 812.

28   Ibid., p. 802.

29   Grant, "Review of Said."

30   Grant, "Celine: Art and Politics," p. 807.

31   Grant, "Faith and the Multiversity," in *Technology and Justice*. (Toronto: House of Anansi Press Limited, 1986), pp. 35-77.

32   Ibid., pp. 45-46.

33   Ibid., p. 47.

34   Ibid., p. 66.

35   Grant, "Interview," July 17, 1988.

36   In his 1951 article "Philosophy," Grant had argued that "Philosophy cannot produce that intuition of the beautiful out of which art arises, but it can help to promote that unity of mind in which such intuitions will best flourish." op.cit. *supra*, p. 132.

37   Grant, *English-Speaking Justice*, p. 1.

38   Grant, "Faith and the Multiversity," *Technology and Justice*, p. 48.

39   Plato, *Phaedo*, 78a. My translation, following H.N. Fowler.